A.E. Wilson Sept
1976

ENGLISH VILLAGES

1 (overleaf) *Castle Combe, Wiltshire*

JOHN BURKE

ENGLISH VILLAGES

B. T. Batsford Ltd
London
and Sydney

For JEAN
who shared the best of the journeys

First published 1975

© John Burke 1975

ISBN 0 7134 2932 1

Printed and bound in Great Britain by
Richard Clay (The Chaucer Press) Ltd, Bungay, Suffolk
for the publishers B. T. Batsford Ltd
4 Fitzhardinge Street
London W1H 0AH
and 23 Cross Street, Brookvale, NSW 2100, Australia

CONTENTS

LIST OF ILLUSTRATIONS

ACKNOWLEDGEMENTS

The author and publishers would like to
thank the following for permission to
reproduce photographs:

Barnaby's Picture Library: Pl. 9
J. Allan Cash: Pls. 8, 15, 17, 22, 25
Noel Habgood, FRPS: Pls. 1, 6, 7, 10, 12, 14, 16, 23
Kenneth Scowen, FIIP, FRPS: Pls. 2, 3, 5, 11, 19, 20, 21, 24
The late Edwin Smith: Pls. 4, 13, 18

ENGLISH VILLAGES

Foundations

Most people have a fairly clear picture of their ideal village. Even the cynical would probably have to admit, being basically as sentimental as the rest of us, that its features bear a strong resemblance to those on picture postcards and glossy calendars. It is all very well to declare a lofty distaste for Castle Combe, Kersey and Broadway: the thousands who flock to see them every year—'hunting after the picturesque like beagles', as Keats put it—do so because the places really do charm the eye, really do have character, and really do represent ways of building and retain echoes of a way of life which we nostalgically feel may have been preferable to our own.

The picture postcard and our colourful calendar fail to show what the unmade roads must have looked like in the days when those villages were created; nor does the modern visitor feel the ague in his bones or have to brave the stench of interiors which for centuries boasted no running water and no adequate sanitation. To this visitor, as to the collector of coloured 'views', the cottage gardens are always full of summer flowers, the stream beside the village green sparkles in eternal sunshine (and no longer serves as the communal drain), and the only smell is the warm and reassuring one from the bonnet of his car.

The cosiness of some villages and the leisurely sprawl of others can suggest an idyllic age during which all men and women were content with their work and with the social order. Great decisions might be made in the cities, but the noble toil of the farmer and craftsman went on at a measured, more dignified pace in the country. Each community was well-nigh self-sufficient. The farrier, the wheelwright, the butcher and the thatcher each played his part, and sang his part tunefully and respectfully in church or chapel on Sunday. There were no supermarkets a few miles away, no frozen foods and no wrapped, sliced loaves. Many housewives baked at home but those with no oven could rely on getting bread almost as good from

the baker at the end of the lane. He was more than a maker and pur-
veyor of bread : until well into this century many rural families had
no oven or could not afford to fuel the fire too often, so it was no
uncommon thing for the weekend joint to be taken to the bakery and
cooked in the oven there.

At home and at day school or Sunday school, children were
adjured to recite and abide by the promise, 'To do my duty in that
state of life unto which it may please God to call me'. A contributor
to a recent collection of Norfolk Women's Institute reminiscences
confesses that sixty years ago in the village of Shipdham she, being
sensitive about her thinness, used to add a silent prayer of her own :
'But please give me fat legs and drawers with lace on'.

Life was hard and debilitating rather than snug in most rural communities during most periods of their existence. In the eighteenth
century, regarded by many as the most truly golden and gracious
era in English society, Nathaniel Kent had to write :

The shattered hovels which half the poor of this kingdom are
obliged to put up with, is truly affecting to a heart fraught with
humanity. Those who condescend to visit these miserable tene-
ments can testify that neither health or decency can be preserved
in them.

Well into Victorian times the picture shows little improvement or
hope of improvement. In a one-room cottage where the father of a
family had just died from typhus, the doctor reported :

I remember the horse stood at the back of the bed. The stench was
dreadful. In addition to the horse, there were fowls roosting on the
tops of the bedsteads, and I think the family was not under ten
souls. Where there are many children it is common for ten or
twelve people to inhabit one apartment.

It is amazing that so many hamlets and villages have survived, and
survived in their original setting. Plague, border feuds and wars, enclosures and spells of agricultural depression have wiped out whole
settlements; but of the thousands which remain, the majority had

already been established before the Normans came, and are recorded in Domesday Book. What is now picturesque was once severely practical. The weaver's cottage which is today a stockbroker's week-end retreat was put there so that a man might make a living. That trim little row of almshouses beside the village green was not added merely as decoration. As for the village pump, so quaint with its surround of ornamental railings or a tiled roof donated by some twentieth-century benefactor, it could be the most significant feature in the whole scene—the presence of water having dictated the siting of the village in the first place.

In the shape of hamlet or village we see the shape of our entire history, not so much preserved as sketched in and then revised, and revised again. The ground plan of our rude forefathers is interwoven with the handiwork of later invaders or restorers, admirers and despoilers. The shadow of an old doorway reasserts itself through stone or brick in defiance of a new entrance flanked by polished carriage lamps, the name of an inn preserves memories of a battle or a man forgotten by most of us, the hummock supporting the parish church has in the past yielded up traces of an older people and older religion.

Professor W. G. Hoskins puts it, as he does most things, succinctly and irrefutably:

In most parts of England *everything is older than we think.*

According to the likeliest calculations, the land bridge which once linked Britain to Europe was finally inundated between 6000 and 5000 B.C., when water from melted glaciers flowed between what became in due course the French and south-east English coasts. Old Stone Age hunters and, later, farmers had come into the country along the old causeway. By 2500 B.C. New Stone Age colonists were making their way across the Channel, setting up homesteads on the chalk downs or on the south-western moorlands. These encampments were flimsy and impermanent. The newcomers were semi-nomadic, and the evidence they have left of their passing is mainly in the form of causewayed hill forts, earthworks probably supplemented by wooden gates and palisades, which appear to have been used only as

meeting places for religious purposes or as communal defences for
scattered groups threatened by rivals and new waves of immigrants.
We know they brought seed corn and domestic animals with them,
but it was not until the Celts arrived around 1000 B.C. that what
could reasonably be called settlements of any substance were created.

Instead of driving herds from one grazing patch to another, the
Celts set up stock enclosures and laid out fields for systematic agriculture. Organized farming of this kind involved a parallel social
organization, and the birth of the village as we know it. Domestic
crafts had the chance to develop: women made their own pottery
and had the time and incentive for weaving and other occupations.
While itinerant specialists such as bronze and iron smiths might still
wander from one district to another selling their services where
needed, local men learned such skills for themselves and, as it were,
set up shop.

The sites adopted give some idea of prevailing conditions. Bronze
Age and Iron Age villages on the downland ridges were in effect
family farms, with clusters of huts surrounded by pasture and strips
of primitive agriculture. Some kept close to earlier earthworks, or
gradually enlarged their own groups to provide more effective defence against enemies. Many large forts, such as the Trundle near
Goodwood, were occupied at one time and another by a succession
of races and tribes in various stages of development.

In Somerset the defences were of a different kind. Settlers who
chose these marshy lowlands in preference to the heights built their
homesteads on existing or artificial mounds, strengthened with
stones and wood, the individual huts being often raised on stilts to
escape seasonal flooding. Exit and entrance were by means of wooden
causeways to firmer ground, planned for easy resistance to attackers.
Traces of two such settlements have been found preserved in peat at
Godney and Meare. Godney is estimated to have had more than
sixty circular wattle-and-daub huts with thatched roofs, standing
on mounds of wood and clay.

The perishable nature of such building materials means that many
regions have bequeathed us little more than domestic utensils, ornaments and weapons, often fragmented. Some of the Somerset lake

2   *Clovelly, Devon*

village relics are displayed in the Lake Museum at Glastonbury, others in the County Museum at Taunton. Only where enduring stone or massive earthen embankments were used can we find substantial remains above ground. A large part of modern Avebury flanks a main street cutting right through the centre of a circular earthwork and the surviving uprights of a concentric stone circle, with two lesser circles within. Thanks to aerial photography, previously undetected furrows and shadows of lesser constructions are gradually being revealed across the entire country.

Granite has preserved the shape of some foundations in the Land's End peninsula. Chysauster still has walls of its drystone houses set about a courtyard and flanked by a cobbled street, with byres for cattle and some small garden plots. As bolt-holes in time of emergency the inhabitants dug subterranean passages known in Cornwall as fogous. This Iron Age hamlet was occupied until well into the Roman era, its livelihood the tin-mining industry.

In Norfolk an attempt has been made at Cockley Cley to re-create on authentic earthworks an Iceni village as it might have been in A.D. 60 or thereabouts. Ringed by a stockade of local fen and marsh reeds, it contains a chieftain's hut, a long house for the élite of the tribe, a chariot house, and other conjectural buildings. The Iceni, driven into East Anglia by the aggressive expansion of the Trinovantes and the Belgae, are believed to have established their headquarters at Caistor St Edmund, known to the Romans as *Venta Icenorum*, a few miles south of modern Norwich. Imperial historians describe their custom of felling trees to make an outer wall, and the building of huts within that barricade, entered only through one gap with gates or, as at Cockley Cley, a drawbridge over a moat. One reason for the establishment of such a fortification here is still obvious: a cheerfully gushing spring which, even in times of drought, has never ceased to provide fresh water, far more desirable than a well or running stream which men and their animals could in time pollute.

The immediate vicinity of Cockley Cley is a fascinating historical palimpsest. The Icknield Way and the Roman road from Caistor to Stamford crossed here, and only a few hundred yards from the first-

3 *Widecombe-in-the-Moor, Devon*

century village are preserved a fourth-century Roman lead coffin and tiles from a Roman mausoleum, together with the skeleton of a man of the Beaker Folk some four thousand years old, in a fifteenth-century forge converted into a museum. Adjoining this little cottage is the shell of a seventh-century Saxon church, believed to be the oldest in the country, with Danish and Norman additions. After the Reformation this was converted into a home for the parish priest, and was privately occupied until after the Second World War.

Near Stoke Prior in Worcestershire the Avoncroft open-air museum of buildings displays reconstructed Iron Age dwellings, and continues through later centuries with examples of buildings saved from demolition and brought to the site to form a permanent collection of different architectural styles. At Singleton in West Sussex the Weald and Downland museum has similar aims, featuring life-size models of a Saxon weaver's hut, a charcoal burner's camp and a medieval cottage along with a genuine nineteenth-century toll house, a granary, and two fifteenth-century farmhouses saved from a Kent valley doomed to become a reservoir.

In spite of inter-tribal conflicts the Celts consolidated their families and their farms securely enough to be able, after some generations, to produce a surplus of grain for export. Tin miners of the West had throughout the Bronze Age carried on a healthy trade with the rest of Europe and even with merchants from the farther reaches of the Mediterranean, and sporadic attempts were made to exploit also the iron ores of the forbidding Wealden forests of the south-east.

When the Romans came they enforced few changes on the agricultural system of their new colony. While ambitious Britons might adopt Roman customs and eventually obtain promotion into the higher social and administrative circles of the cities, peasant life plodded on much as before. Isolated family farms and nucleated settlements well meriting the name of village existed side by side with—or perhaps it would be truer to say at a respectful distance from—the Romanized complexes known as villas. These were the preserve of what today we would call gentlemen farmers: some of them then, as today, retired army officers. Lullingstone in Kent seems to have been the country house of a part-time arable farmer, with

4 *Dunster, Somerset*

Belgic open fields or 'lynchets' on the neighbouring slopes, and the later addition of a tannery and a huge grain store. At Bignor in Sussex the owner is more likely to have gone in for extensive sheep ranching than tilling the fields. Both sets of buildings, like the fragments of others which have come to light, were luxuriously appointed: there were bathrooms, central heating, and exquisite mosaic floors; a temple and mausoleum at Lullingstone, a banqueting hall and enclosed courtyard with a roofed-in walk at Bignor.

Centres such as London, York and Chichester continue to disgorge impressive Romano-British remains, which is only to be expected in view of their size and consequence. What can often be more exciting is the revelation of ancient foundations beneath an apparently innocuous little village. Rewarding discoveries of this kind were made early in the nineteenth century when the local squire encouraged excavations in and around the Yorkshire village of Aldborough, close to the Great North Road (now the A1) but happily insulated from it.

The village itself is a glowing slope of gracefully proportioned houses down to a village green complete with tall maypole. Whether approached downhill or from the little twists of road beyond the green, it offers one little shock of pleasure after another. Just as it stands it is a delight. But there is more to it than this attractive surface: its back gardens, its church, and the manor house are all locked inextricably into the walls and sunken floors and streets of not just one older Aldborough, but at least two.

Here once stood Iseur, stronghold of the warrior Brigantes, headquarters perhaps of that very queen who betrayed Caractacus to the Romans. Taken over by the invaders as *Isurium Brigantum*, it became a key post on the road between Hadrian's Wall and York. Its outer wall cuts through the fabric of the eighteenth-century manor and across the pleasantly shaded grounds behind the museum. Four gates are identifiable, and the foundations of the watch-towers. A path skirting the back gardens of cottages and the village pub leads to a couple of small sheds protecting tessellated pavements, while horses in an adjacent paddock watch with some disdain the comings and goings of earnest students.

5 *Corfe Castle, Dorset*

In the museum are fragments unearthed from this imperial past. As usual, the smallest objects are the most appealing in their immediate, vivid evocation of the everyday life of our predecessors on a human scale—pins and ornaments, a razor, a bronze back-scratcher. There is an altar top dedicated to Jupiter and the Mother Goddesses, and Mercury has actually brazened his way on to a panel in the church, accompanying its roll of Christian incumbents.

A little way out of the village on a by-road to Boroughbridge stand even more ancient symbols. Three millstone grit monoliths, the biggest just over twenty feet tall, are lined up along a span of nearly six hundred feet leading directly towards what was once a ford across the River Ure. It is all too easy to speculate about their astronomical or ritual significance, in tune with the Stonehenge theories, or to associate them with the 'leys' over which there has been so much controversy. Local folklore has it that they were hurled by the devil at Aldborough in an attempt to destroy the place, and so they have come to be known as The Devil's Arrows. Fortunately he missed.

Towns, villas and villages were left unprotected when troops were recalled to counter barbarian attacks on Rome itself. Educated Britons, accustomed to the well-regulated Roman civilization and to its military backing and discipline, lacked the power to stand up for themselves and their property, and soon lost heart in the face of Anglo-Saxon invasions. The peasants, never in the mainstream of Romano-British culture, either waited apprehensively for the barbarian influx or did some plundering of the more vulnerable towns on their own account.

Between the middle of the sixth century and the middle of the seventh, the Anglo-Saxons shared out almost the whole country. Their settlements were markedly different from those which had gone before. Though their tribal groupings relied on a strong family element, they did not huddle together quite as the Celts had done, and chose the lowlands rather than the hilltops for their villages. Some of these 'tuns' had huts spaced out along lanes and paths within a stockade, changing the habits of those forebears of whom Tacitus had scornfully observed: 'They do not even tolerate houses built

in rows. They dwell apart and at a distance from each other, according to the preference they may have for the stream, the plain or
the grove.' But these new methods were in no way a tribute to the
orderliness of the intervening Roman civilization. Most of the grid-
pattern towns and other remains of Romano-British times were
shunned by the invaders. They did not even make much use of the
brick and stone to strengthen their own houses. 'They make no use
of stone cut from the quarry, or of tiles,' Tacitus further noted :
'for every sort of building they use unshapely wood.' This accusation
was still valid, though not all their constructions could be called
unshapely. Where the Celts had been satisfied with conical struc-
tures or tent-like formations of branches, reeds and straw plastered
together over a light ridge pole, the Saxons aimed at something
stronger. The chieftain and his favoured entourage spent much of
their time in a great central hall supported on solid timbers and
with properly pegged, properly stressed roofs. There might be a
number of other substantial buildings in the enclave; but it appears
to have been true that the lower orders did little better than previous
generations of British peasants, if the excavations near Sutton
Courtenay of sunken rectangles are anything to go by, covered as
they must have been by little more than simple sapling and brushwood frameworks resting on low mud walls.

Those Celts who had not been massacred or taken into servitude
retreated to the west and there reverted to their old system of
lonely farmsteads or small groupings. In some fringe areas their
hilltop communities survived in wary amity alongside, but above,
the lowland Saxons.

As communities grew and turbulent minor chieftains fell under
the sway of a smaller number of powerful regional kings such as
Alfred of Wessex, the forms of the nucleated village as we know
them began to emerge and solidify. A few hilltop villages may have
survived, altered and over-built, from earlier days; but most existing
sites and names, apart from new growths or a shift of population
caused by the Industrial Revolution, are the work of the Anglo-
Saxons and their immediate followers and enemies, the Norsemen.
Even when we come across a place with the prefix 'New', the chances

are that this newness relates to the late Saxon or early Norman period.

Cottages in our favourite beauty spots may vary widely in appearance and building materials, from the stone of the Cotswolds to the half-timbering of the Midlands and the Weald, but the villages themselves fall basically into only three or four categories. There is the green village; the thoroughfare or street village; the so-called 'heap' village dumped down about a road junction; and the formless hamlet or village which at first glance seems, like Topsy, to have 'just growed'. The third of these types can, of course, have much in common with either the second or the fourth, and some purists would deny it any separate existence, preferring to classify it with one of the others.

The first type is the one which we can perhaps most readily visualize. All villages worthy of the name must surely have a village green, just as they must have a duckpond, a church and an old inn with a log fire and an inglenook? In fact the distribution of such settlements can be a lengthy study in itself, conditioned by the predominance of certain farming methods in certain localities, the need for defence against enemies, and the configurations of the countryside. One thing is certain: picturesque as it may be now, the village green, whether it be broad or narrow, flat or sloping, square or triangular, came into being for purely aesthetic reasons just about as frequently as did the parish pump.

Many a green would originally have been used for grazing, before the encroachment of later houses and wider highways, and may have been much bigger than it is now: big enough to be virtually the village common, as in many spacious Suffolk villages and several in Surrey, and big enough to house travelling fairs and any number of communal sports and activities. The villagers of the past would have had scant sympathy for their successors who 'want to keep Little Twitterden the way it always was' by banning boy footballers, courting couples, and such excrescences as swings and roundabouts from the sward.

In northern England the green village had all too often to be conceived as an embattled encampment. The houses formed a stockade, the green was a refuge for beasts hurried in from open grazing lands when threatened by Scottish raiders. Roads into the centre could be sealed off by lydgates. Heighington in County Durham is a classic example, and it is interesting to consider the near certainty that the church and churchyard, breaching what was obviously the original contour of the green, must in spite of their age be younger than that green. The towers of such churches, like the pele towers of parsonages and manor houses along the Border, played an essential part as refuges and lookout posts.

It is rare to find a street village in the harassed areas of the Border counties. A long-drawn-out string of buildings had none of the protective capability of a compact settlement where the houses themselves formed a stubborn square about the heart of the place.

Street villages are, by definition, those which flowered beside busy thoroughfares. Whereas most of us today would prefer our home to be set well back from the traffic of the main road, great numbers of villages owed their survival to that traffic. As well as the main artery the inhabitants usually, in common with those of the green villages, created a back lane—frequently called just that to this day. Running behind the houses and outhouses of the cheek-by-jowl smallholdings, the lane gave access to paths leading off past the arable fields of the community to common grazing land beyond. It was often linked to the main street by a minor lane at each end of the village, and in due course by more modern side streets as the place expanded and a few old properties obligingly fell down or were knocked down.

Long Melford in Suffolk is one of the most splendid street villages, though it also boasts a green, not as an enclosed feature but rather as an appendage, sloping up from the extreme end of the village to the glorious flushwork of its church while the main road drives on towards Bury St Edmunds. Another famous name is that of Stilton, a Huntingdonshire venue for Leicestershire farmers taking their cheeses for collection and delivery by stage coach to London. Once an important staging post on the Great North Road, Stilton is now by-passed by a loop of the AI. The great coaching inns are, not surprisingly, to be found right by the roadside in such villages rather than tucked away in a secluded corner of some green village: drivers and passengers on the expresses had little time for the turns and twists of narrow side lanes. Long Melford has its *Bull*, Stilton its *Bell*.

Such communities inevitably developed a plumper physique if set at a crossroads. Dwellings then spread along any of the four approach roads and eventually filled in the angles, with shorter byways cutting across these corners. As a region prospered and improved communications became essential, as in the various stages of industrialization, a street village which had hitherto relied on north–south trade might find itself being converted into a new entity by the laying of an east–west road to open up, literally, new avenues of trade and transport.

The hardest communities to define, and in many ways the most interesting to examine, are the formless villages. Settlers opening up clearings in the forest or squatters on patches of common land might for years remain separated from their nearest neighbours and then, willingly or unwillingly, be linked by a path trodden more and more decisively into a regular thoroughfare. Scattered hamlets were gradually joined by roads and an infilling of individual homesteads to produce a shapeless yet loosely co-ordinated community. One of them might be senior or substantial enough to establish a mother church and ultimately impose its own name on the associated hamlets. Some villages grew by the haphazard or calculated addition of more houses within their own confines; others by spawning a hamlet which kept its distance yet maintained a working relationship with the parent.

The foundation dates of villages can be estimated fairly accurately from their names, even when spelling and pronunciation have been distorted by the linguistic foibles of later occupants.

Few Celtic place names survive save in the extreme west, though a number can still be recognized in certain river names such as the Thames, the Tarrant, the Dove and the Derwent. Celtic influences in the west can be identified in such formations as *Tre*, a settlement; *Lan*, a sacred enclosure or a church; *Pen* or *Bray*, a hill; *Caer*, a camp. Many Welsh words also have the same roots. Grantchester is probably Celtic, formed by the addition of the familiar Roman *castra* to the name of the River Granta.

That there are so few villages of whose Celtic origin we can be absolutely certain may be due to the fact that so few were ever of sufficient consequence to survive, even without the Anglo-Saxon takeover. When the conquerors did, rarely, make use of an existing site they might adopt its existing name also, but this was refashioned to suit their own tongue, and Norman French influences duly led to further mutation. On the whole the new residents preferred to attach their own descriptions to both old and new settlements. The spread of Anglo-Saxon control of the country can be traced through the successive implications of these names.

The earliest footholds are defined by the ending *-ingas*, as in Hastings, Godalming, Barking and Oving. This meant 'descendants of' or, in a wider sense, 'people of' the relevant chieftains: the Haestingas were followers of Haesten, who founded a community between the Kentings and the South Saxons; Godalming was the place of Godhelm's people, Pickering that of the people of Picer. *Ham* is clearly related to a homestead or village, as in Caterham, Westerham and Longham. Compounded, these two suffixes produce more detailed identification of a site, establishing Effingham as the homestead of the people of Effa, Rockingham as the homestead of Hroca's people.

Tun or *ton* is the genesis of our own 'town'. The complicated Ruyton-of-the-Eleven-Towns in Shropshire can probably be translated as 'the rye-growing settlement of the eleven hamlets'. *Hurst*, as in Goudhurst or Brockenhurst, referred to woodland. Very common in Kent is the ending *-den*, referring to a clearing cut out of forest land in order to pasture swine. Smarden, Horsmonden, Benenden, Rolvenden, Bethersden . . . the list is endless. Progress in clearing these breaks in the great 'wild' of the Weald was so slow that most of the names are recorded only a little while before the Norman Conquest.

Equally common in the Fens and marshlands are references to features as significant in that landscape as the woods and clearings were in the south-east: *-eg*, *-ey* or *-ea* denote an island, which might be no more than a hummock which remained dry and solid above the waterlogged levels and so could be cultivated and built on.

Some confusions are inevitable. The ending *-hamm* implies water meadows, but has often been truncated to *-ham* and therefore mis-leadingly suggests a homestead. Old English *-wic* or *-wick* can mean a market-place or, more frequently, a dairy farm—Butterwick and Chiswick must have had a good reputation for butter and cheese. But the Norsemen used *-wick* to define a coastal inlet, whence the dreaded name of the Vikings.

Danes and Norwegians left their clearest imprints on the northern regions of England. *By*, in modern Danish a town, in the past identi-fied a sizeable farmstead or village and was sometimes preceded by a personal name as in Arkleby and Scratby, sometimes by mention of a natural feature as in Raby (the homestead by the boundary mark) or Linby, in Nottinghamshire (by the lime tree). A lesser settlement, such as a hamlet set apart from the main community, might incorporate *-thorpe*; though, just to confuse the issue once more, the Anglo-Saxons had a similar word. To sum up far more arbitrarily than the subject merits, we may say that the Danelaw in the north-east and the Norse settlements of the north-west added to our language such forms as *-toft*, the site of a homestead, often with the owner's name attached, as in Knaptoft; *-holm* or *-hulme*, an island; *-thwaite* for a clearing, like the Norse hamlet of Stonethwaite in Borrowdale; and everyday words such as gill, breck and beck.

The Normans, whose main body of fighting men had in any case so much Norse blood, never imposed their French dialect on the common people of England. But their rule was marked by some conversions or distortions of place names, here and there by a Norman French addition to a previous description. *Beau* or *bea*, meaning beautiful, became a not infrequent prefix. The 'home on the hill' of Dunham in Cheshire acquired the name of Harvo de Masei, rewarded by the Conqueror with a barony for his support in the invasion, to make it Dunham Massey. A couple of sheep farms known simply as Shepton now also took on the names of knights to whom they had been granted, becoming Shepton Beauchamp and Shepton Mallet. Malpas in Cheshire signified a difficult way. Montacute in Somerset and Egremont, found both in Cumbria and in the Wirral, have an identical meaning: a sharp-pointed hill.

More far-reaching than verbal variations were the changes the Normans brought about in the social pattern. The introduction of their feudal system laid stern obligations upon baron and villager alike. The lord of the manor held his estates from the king and in return promised such military or other services as the king might require. In his turn the lord sub-let lands and granted certain privileges to subordinates, and through them exercised a rough-and-ready code of justice and employment for the peasantry—who farmed the lands, carried out such menial duties as were required, and provided an allotted number of fighting men when the king called for them. The lower ranks in this hierarchy supplied much and received little. Their 'security' was the security of virtual slaves who would not be allowed to starve only because they were more useful when alive.

On taking up a sub-tenancy, a lesser functionary had to make an entry payment; and thereafter to pay many dues in kind. Even a supposed 'free man' found it inadvisable to move from one master to another, and was rarely free in the sense of being utterly independent. Lower down the scale, a villein could rarely accumulate enough to buy anything worth while, least of all his freedom. Legislators of the time might argue over the distinction between a free and non-free servitor as an intellectual exercise, but in reality there were few chances of escape: a villein could not buy his freedom since it was part of the whole feudal philosophy that he possessed nothing which was not in effect his overlord's. There were dues payable on marriage; and, in order to retain an adequate work force on the estate, an especially severe penalty was levied on any man whose daughter wished to marry out of the community—a financial burden which few could afford, any more than they could afford their master's displeasure.

Many a village which had flourished in Saxon times was destroyed during the Conqueror's merciless 'harrying of the North'. Others disappeared as a result of his passion for hunting. 'The forest has its own laws', wrote William's royal treasurer, Richard Fitz-Nigel,

'based not on the common law of the realm, but on arbitrary legislation by the king.' Arbitrary it undoubtedly was. In vast reserves
set aside for the chase, savage game laws were enacted, old usages
abrogated and existing communities driven out. Greatnam and
Hartford in the New Forest were only two examples among many of
summary depopulation. There must have been great, if mute, satisfaction among many dispossessed homesteaders when the Conqueror's successor, William Rufus, met his mysterious death from an
arrow near the present village of Minstead. The presumed scene of his
downfall is marked by a stone donated in 1745 by Earl De La Warr.

Forest clearings and pastures were awarded early on to the new
king's henchmen, subject always to his own ultimate control and
continuing approval. There was no more free squatting, no more
growth of self-reliant hamlets and villages.

William's devout encouragement of monastic influence throughout the land was another factor in the destruction of villages.
The Cistercians in particular sought solitude for their abbeys—
and also plenty of space for profitable sheep-walks. Whole communities were banished, though in some cases help was provided
to re-establish them at a suitable distance.

Sheep were the basis of the most important national industry
right through the Middle Ages. In its infancy the production of wool
could well be called a 'cottage industry', for many processes could
be carried out by individuals in their own homes. Flemish weavers
came into England from the twelfth century onwards, and immigration was intensified by Edward III's invitation to more of them to
settle and teach their 'mysteries' to the English, so that finished
cloth could be produced here instead of the raw material having to
be exported for manufacture abroad. Their influence was shown not
only in the development of weaving techniques but in agricultural
imports and methods—they had a lot to teach about market gardening, and brought with them a species of cherry which became famous
as the 'Kentish' cherry—and in architectural styles which in due
course appeared in many buildings in the south-east, such as the
attractive cottages of Sarre, and in much of East Anglia.

Norfolk and Suffolk were the most flourishing centres for the clothiers. Worstead, an attractive little grouping of Georgian and Queen Anne houses near North Walsham, with an imposing medieval church, gave its name to a fine woollen yarn. In the exquisite village of Kersey, swooping down through its little watersplash and up again to another great church, originated a coarser fabric known as Kersey-mere, and Lindsey Woolsey came from the neighbouring village of Lindsey. By the late fourteenth century one-fifth of the male population of Hadleigh was engaged in the industry. The richness of villages in this region, prouder and more sumptuous than many a town three or four times their size, is owed mainly to the weavers and the great wool merchants. Suffolk's mighty churches, whose parishes could never have supplied an adequate congregation, came into being as a sort of prosperous clothiers' premium on some heavenly insurance policy.

Heavily committed to this one specialized craft, the working population of East Anglia suffered a severe depression when trade drifted away to the west. This came about with the invention of fulling machines worked by water instead of by foot. Streams were more plentiful and more powerful in the Cotswolds, which also had suitable deposits of fuller's earth for use in cleansing the fabric. The stone cottages of the west are as attractive to sightseers as the timbered homes and workshops of the eastern weavers. There are as many memorial tributes to clothiers in the 'wool churches' of the Cotswolds as in those of Lavenham and district. The terraced levels of Chalford, perched on the side of the Frome valley in Gloucestershire, look the way they do because of their relation to brooks and springs where yarn was washed; and there are dozens of other villages who lineaments can best be interpreted in relation to the local industry.

Even the beginnings of the Industrial Revolution did not immediately do away with the need for the cottage weaver. Looms driven by water power came into use in the West Country and along the Pennines, but there was still plenty of work for the operative in his own home, with his own plot of land and his own preferences for allocation of working hours. Heptonstall in Yorkshire began as a collection of individual weavers with their living-rooms and workrooms high on a hill. Then water-powered looms began to operate in the valley, and the township of Hebden Bridge formed. Steam power put paid to the Cotswold tradition, and irrevocably altered the pattern elsewhere. Concentrated around the Pennine coalfields, small villages grew up in the vicinity of small factories; but the factories grew larger, and just as watermills had given way to steam engines so the villages had either to grow hurriedly—and grimly—into mechanized textile towns, or crumble into dereliction. A gulf widened between the country craftsman and the industrial labourer, between villager and townsman.

While all these changes were taking place, however, and while pestilence and dynastic and political battles raged intermittently through the land, agriculture was still for centuries the mainstay of most of the population. Villages expanded as production expanded, exports of corn contributed to national prosperity as surely as exports of wool and cloth; and after the decline of the feudal system most country folk had some use of common land for grazing their own beasts and for the supply of brushwood and turf as fuel.

Across what was, by and large, a reasonably well balanced economy in the middle of the fourteenth century swept the Black Death. Within two years at least a million people—some say up to half the population—died, and many a village was utterly abandoned. The surviving peasants sought higher wages. Farmers and landowners, with a smaller and more expensive labour force at their disposal, sought methods of increasing productivity and cutting down the number of hands needed to implement it. Whatever other problems may change over the centuries, this management/manpower one remains pretty consistent.

Many landowners abandoned arable farming and cleared fields and villages to provide sheep-walks. Others, though continuing in agriculture, considered that the farming of innumerable small open strips by families and groups of villagers was inefficient, and that the presence of great tracts of untilled common land was a luxury which could no longer be condoned. As the population increased again, and towns grew, more and more food was needed. Inevitably there was an element of greed in the decisions of many squires who urged the structural revision of the countryside. Given Parliamentary approval for the enclosure and exploitation of wasteland, and with only bewildered, uninstructed villagers to cope with, they found little difficulty in turning what had once been common land into their own private demesnes. The introduction of hedges or walls of local stone to contain fields large and small created the patchwork which we are accustomed to think of as the truly characteristic English landscape.

With a smaller work force needed on the newly 'rationalized' land and with their own smallholdings cut down and their free grazing snatched from them, many cottagers could not survive. Villages shrank. Village craftsmen and unskilled labourers alike moved to the towns, which were greedy for employees. Even those villages which remained viable tended to lose the very men who had most to offer the community. With his enclosed farmland now some way from his home village, the small farmer who could afford it was inclined to move out and build a new farmhouse beside his place of work. The effects of this are especially noticeable in the Midlands, where large farmhouses of the Georgian period stand as remote and stately as some well-wrought wayside chapel far across the fields. Old dwellings left in the village street were often divided into two or three separate cottages, only to be knocked back together again in modern times by those seeking genuine olde-worlde property but not wishing that genuineness to be, by contemporary standards, claustrophobic and cramped.

Further destruction of villages took place when eighteenth-century aristocracy and the rising gentry wished to surround their country homes with fashionable parkland and vistas unmarred by the cottages of the poor. In some cases they were enlightened enough to provide new villages outside the walls of the expanded park or in some alternative setting, often made from better materials and to a better plan. One appealing example is that of Milton Abbas in Dorset. Other benevolent ventures include Blanchland in Northumberland, built by Lord Crewe for his workers, and the estate village of Wimpole in Cambridgeshire, completely refashioned in the middle of the nineteenth century.

Isolated gestures of this kind did little to preserve the way of life in the majority of villages. Between the 1760s and 1860s Parliamentary enclosures amounted to some seven million acres, and although villagers had been promised that they would be granted adequate garden allotments to make up for the loss of grazing and other rights, no more than a token gesture was made in this direction. A succession of agricultural slumps brought poverty and starvation close to many a doorstep. Not everybody wanted to pull up his roots and work in a dark, soulless city; but every man wanted at least to make his own honest living in the place to which he belonged. In 1830 there was a revolt of labourers across southern England and up through the Midlands and East Anglia, supposedly under the command of an unidentifiable 'Captain Swing'. Ricks were set on fire, newly introduced threshing machines destroyed. The demonstrators wanted higher wages and more generous poor law relief, and a reduction in their rents and tithe demands. The outbreak was savagely repressed, nine men hanged, over four hundred sentenced to transportation and hundreds of others to imprisonment. Well might a sort of 'folk blues' of its day lament:

> *We labour hard from morn to night until*
> *our bones do ache,*
> *Then everyone they must obey, their mouldy*
> *beds must make.*
> *We often wish, when we lay down, we ne'er*
> *may rise no more*
> *To meet our savage Governors upon Van*
> *Diemen's shore.*

Conditions in the dark satanic mills might be bad, but could they conceivably be worse than those on the land?

It was not until the drift towards the industrial towns had become a rush that legislation was hurried through to provide country folk with some inducement to remain in the country. More promises were made about the provision of allotments, and a number of measures culminated in the Small Holdings and Allotments Act of 1908. By then the whole balance of English life had altered irreparably.

The villages which have come into being since Domesday Book in 1086 have done so largely because of the incidence of specialized trades and industries or advances in transport and communication. Others of older lineage, already ekeing out a limited rural existence, might suddenly find themselves transported into a bustling new age by the arrival of a canal, a turnpike, or a main railway line. Stourport did not exist until James Brindley added his Staffordshire and Worcestershire canal to the junction of the Stour and Severn, and set up wharves and warehouses there. It mushroomed into a town of some consequence and, indeed, of some elegance; with the decline of the canal trade, and despite its later industrial development, its waterside kernel has reverted to something remarkably 'villagey' in atmosphere. Shardlow in Derbyshire grew and declined for similar reasons. Stoke Bruerne on the Grand Junction Canal in Northamptonshire, with its hump-back bridge and staircase of locks, has a little museum of barge and canal mementoes. Melton Constable in Norfolk aspired to become another Ashford or Crewe with its railway works, but now even the station has been shut down, and if the village is remembered it is more likely to be on account of Sir Jacob Astley, who built himself Melton Hall and at the battle of Edgehill uttered the famous prayer, 'O Lord, Thou knowest how busy I must be this day : if I forget Thee, do not Thou forget me'.

The gorge of the Severn near Coalbrookdale is rich in memories of the early ironfounder, Abraham Darby, with the first iron bridge which gave its name to a village soon to become a small town and ultimately the springboard of the new conurbation of Telford. In Ironbridge Gorge Museum are assembled chapters which draw together hamlets and factories, cottages and furnaces into the story of the Industrial Revolution.

Yet it is misleading to give capital letters to such a phrase, as if there had been just one specific revolution to change the face of the country and the world. Social and industrial change have been continuing processes, sometimes advancing in fits and starts and sometimes accelerating violently, but rarely coming to any lengthy pause. Smoky nineteenth-century towns do not tell the whole story; rarely even begin to tell it. Cromford in Derbyshire remains small—

but it was here that Richard Arkwright first got his cotton spinning frame into significant production, here that he built one of the first factory villages for his workers, and here that the terminal of the remarkable High Peak Railway was established. Sticklepath in Devon preserves water-powered tilt hammers and other machinery associated with busy days of corn and cloth milling and with an early tool factory and grinding house. The steam engine was first securely established in remote Cornish tin mines, and was first moved along rails of the Penydarren tram-road by Richard Trevithick, son of the hamlet of Illogan. Killingworth, today a scheduled new town on the outskirts of Newcastle-upon-Tyne, was a place of no great size when Robert Stephenson carried the principle of the locomotive a stage further. The Fens were conquered and kept under control not from towns set warily about the perimeter but from the likes of Denver and Stretham—Stretham with its beam pumping engine now cared for like a respected cart-horse or pit pony put out to graze in gratitude for past labours, but still capable of pulling its weight in time of emergency.

No one man can hope in his lifetime to learn all the stories and secrets of every village in England. If I am to have the impertinence to act as guide to a chosen few among the many, I may also allow myself the impertinence of dividing them up into categories which appeal to me rather than to other people's ideas of a possibly more logical progression. In extenuation I must plead that all attempted regional sub-divisions, geological bases or historical relationships are filled with contradictions, and hope my chapters are no more absurd than any other potential arrangement.

A sound case can be made out for classifying English villages according to the geological strata on which they stand. After all, their appearance does owe so much to the stone beneath the local soil and to the timber or lack of timber on that soil. We might plausibly relate villages and hamlets along the oolitic limestone belt which leaves Dorset via the Cotswolds and curves up into Lincolnshire, or make valid comparisons between the timbered buildings of the Weald and those of Warwickshire. Rainfall, mountain ranges and rivers frequently make nonsense of county boundaries. But in

6 *Askerswell, Dorset*

spite of the irrelevance of these boundaries, overrun so many times in our history and all too easily wrenched into fresh administrative conformations in 1974, we still visualize the layout of our country most easily in such divisions. I have therefore bunched counties together under what I trust are tolerably appropriate headings.

But what, someone will ask, is Oxfordshire doing in that motley Thamesside and Midland crew when it has so much in common with the West Country? Indeed, since the Thames itself rises in Gloucestershire, would it not be more sensible to . . . ?

And doesn't Lincolnshire have as many affinities with Yorkshire as with East Anglia, and therefore . . . ?

And so on.

A choice has to be made, and if in making it I offend some wiser reader's sense of what is seemly, I apologize; and hope that the waywardness will be provocative rather than merely irritating.

CHAPTER TWO

The Seaboard

The tower of St Senana's church, the westernmost in England, is not large but it is certainly formidable. Braced by granite blocks against the Atlantic winds it seems, like many other buildings on the Land's End peninsula, to be an indestructible outcrop of the rock itself. Sands in Sennen Cove below are golden and welcoming, but up here the world can look very grey and bleak; though within the stubborn little church is a warming, consoling fragment of a sculpture of the Virgin and Child.

Zennor, a little way up the north coast, also owes its name to St Senana, and like Down St Mary in Devon has a mermaid on one of its bench ends. The sea is ever present, beating in on both sides of the peninsula. A few fishing villages straggle down to the shores of sheltered coves, but most consider it wiser to cling to vertiginous slopes above the tide and to armour themselves with solid harbour walls—or, better still, to choose a natural shelter such as some cleft in the rock.

A large slab juts up not far from Sennen church, associated with the legendary hero whose name recurs in every part of this region and far away across the heartlands of England. Known as the Table Men rock, it is supposed to have been the scene of a thanksgiving feast after King Arthur and the combined forces of some Cornish chieftains had defeated a Danish attack.

The nobility of Arthur's deeds is, unfortunately, not the only tradition associated with the coasts of Cornwall and Devon. The Sennen fishermen were once notorious for piracy, watching for foreign ships as eagerly as they watched for pilchard shoals, and sending out many a boarding party to seize gold or goods on their way to and from Ireland. On the island of Lundy, west of Woolacombe, the remains of Marisco Castle commemorate a pirate family who literally ruled the island.

Wreckers, too, have left their sinister shadow across many a bay and village. Ships hammered by an Atlantic gale were all too often driven helplessly into the jagged headlands and unyielding granite of the cliffs. Officially the remains of such wrecks were the property of the local lords of the manor, provided no living creature got ashore to maintain any contrary claim. The local dignitaries were, in these circumstances, not too scrupulous about saving life; and the men of the fishing villages even less so if they could get there first. In 1772 a woman who managed to escape from a shipwreck near Bantham in Devon contrived also to save her jewellery and bedeck herself with it in the belief that this would impress any rough natives she met. It did: she was murdered and stripped of her possessions. In addition to such windfalls the coastal poor were not averse to shaking the tree a little. From leaving a warning beacon unlit it was no great step to contriving false beacons which would lure ships directly on to the rocks. These murderous practices were not as widespread as novelists and other romancers would like to make out; but there is little doubt that in such lawless regions, in a cruel age, they existed.

The sea could prove just as brutal to the villagers as it was to the voyager. If we choose to follow first the north coast of the peninsula, we come beyond the Camel estuary to the attractive little holiday resort of Portquin or Port Quinn. It looks bright and busy enough on a summer's day, but for many decades it was sad and deserted. During a storm in 1697 more than thirty fishermen, mainstay of the small community, were drowned. Their families dispersed, leaving only ghosts to range the streets and harbour.

A couple more miles take us to Port Isaac, one of several seaside villages whose narrow streets have sensibly been banned to traffic. Before the acquisition of a fast inshore rescue boat the village had a larger, conventional lifeboat which had to be dragged by a chain of volunteer helpers between the tightly packed cottages. One local thoroughfare is appropriately known as Squeeze-belly Alley. King Arthur is with us again. Just outside the village is the site of the castle where Uther Pendragon is said to have killed the Earl of Cornwall whose wife he desired, and on whom he fathered the boy destined to be Arthur.

And so, on to Tintagel. Its fourteenth-century post office is more authentic than the hall in which the Arthurian knights are represented in stained glass, though of course it has not been issuing stamps and old age pensions for all these hundreds of years. A miniature manor house, it was opened as a letter receiving office in 1844 to replace the services of a messenger who had hitherto walked to and from Camelford with the mail.

As for the story of King Arthur being both born and killed there, 'tis a piece of tradition, only on oral history, and not any authority to be produced for it.

So said Daniel Defoe of the castle above the village, and above the so-called Merlin's Cave. It is in fact impossible to relate the present ruins in any way to the period when the Romano-British warrior we associate with Arthur fought his rearguard actions against the invading Saxons. There are some traces of Roman occupation in the district, and on Tintagel Head itself there was a Celtic monastery. No mention is made in Domesday Book of any castle, but a Norman style motte and bailey were put in hand some time after 1141 when Reginald, an illegitimate son of Henry i, was created Earl of Cornwall. It was strengthened about a century later, but fell into decay during the fifteenth and sixteenth centuries, and was neglected until nineteenth-century devotees of Tennyson revived interest in it, and the ruins were shored up.

Legends of every kind cling persistently to the houses and headlands of this land beyond the Tamar—a land which the Cornishmen themselves regard as belonging to a different order of being from the rest of humankind. The story of the Forrabury bells, however, has some counterparts in other counties. Here the bells which supposedly ring every now and then from beneath the waves were originally destined for St Symphorian's church, a Norman building with an eighteenth-century tower. The crew bringing them in by sea had a dispute with their captain, who used foul language in the presence of the holy bells, thereby calling down on himself a tempest which sank the ship with all hands. One thinks of the bell which the Danes carried off from Bosham in Sussex and which drowned them all by cracking through the bottom of the boat and sinking into the Bell Hole, from which it still adds its tenor voice to the peal in the church tower; and of the sunken churches and monasteries off Dunwich in Suffolk, ringing a carillon for fishermen on calm nights.

Nearby Boscastle has a museum of witchcraft and sorcery, complete with the implements of the trade and a 'charm well'. Dogs are allowed only on a lead—presumably so that resident familiars are not disturbed—and admission is 'subject to VAT', which conjures up a happy picture of warlocks filling in their Customs and Excise forms with percentages on services rendered and deductible percentages on raw materials. How, one wonders, has inflation affected bats, toads and jumbo-size cauldrons?

Boscastle harbour is one of the wary ones. It is almost landlocked, but to be on the safe side has extended two defensive arms against sudden attack. Sir Richard Grenville rebuilt the inner jetty in 1584. The outer jetty was established early in the nineteenth century, and blown up this century by a Second World War mine, to be restored later by the National Trust. The harbour, together with the harbour-master's house, the old forge and old lime kiln, and large areas of the Valency valley slopes, all come under the jurisdiction of the National Trust. It would be unfair to call the place a museum piece, but it is hard to visualize it as the commercial port it was once meant to be. The harbour was created to handle exports of slate from Delabole quarry, the largest of its kind in England. Its grey-blue slates are as characteristic of Cornwall as the granite blocks and lime-washed walls, the smaller varieties being known as 'peggies' because they were once hung by oak pegs instead of, as nowadays, from nails.

North of the harbour the cliffs rise to the heights of Cambeak, with Crackington Haven tucked comfortably in below. On either side of Bude the sands and hilltop walks have their holiday devotees, but remember rougher and tougher days. Morwenstow was the home both of wreckers and of smugglers. The Reverend Robert Stephen Hawker, who wrote the Song of the Western Men—'And shall Trelawny die?'—inveighed from the pulpit against the wreckers who disgraced his parish, and built himself a wooden hut overlooking the sea, supposedly as a study, but perhaps also to keep an eye on his savage flock. The eccentric chimneys of his old rectory are copies of church towers which he had admired when serving in other incumbencies. Local smugglers were organized by a mysterious stranger known as Cruel Coppinger, who had been saved from a shipwreck by a local girl whom he married and sadistically maltreated. It was said that he was Danish, but he seemed very much at home in the region and soon had all the 'free traders' under his thumb. When the Revenue officers summoned enough strength to defeat the gang in a head-on battle and take possession of their cave in the cliff, Coppinger was rescued by a ship which appeared off the spot where he had originally landed and now spirited him away. Smuggling was even more common on the southern coast of the county, with its strong family ties with the Bretons: Mevagissey, for example, was noted for its production of fast vessels designed specially for the trade, not so much custom built as anti-Customs built.

Clovelly is another of those precipitous villages jammed into narrow combes which insist that you leave your car outside and walk. Here it is no question of local by-laws but of necessity: no wheeled vehicle would risk the steeply descending cobbled steps of the main street. Even in the narrows of this lurching slope, staggering down to the minute harbour, the cottages contrive to sprout tiny terraces and verandas and to enrich them with a luxuriance of flowers. If the journey back uphill is too daunting, you can always hire a donkey and pretend—which is not difficult in this ambience—that you are in Italy or Spain.

Spain, though, is a country whose relationships with the gallant navigators and fighting men of this coast were historically none too friendly. After the success of Charles Kingsley's *Westward Ho!* it was a bright idea on someone's part to bestow the name on a commercially calculated resort, marking the rapid expansion of a profitable tourist trade in the region during Victorian times.

To save many unspoilt stretches of coastline and moorland from future exploitation, the National Trust have taken over as much open country as they and their supporters can afford. A recent acquisition is more than 250 acres near Combe Martin, including the great landmark of Devon's north coast, the Great Hangman, adding another link to the coastal footpath which the more energetic would like to be able to follow from Cornwall right through Devon and on into Somerset.

Like Boscastle, Porlock Weir once had ambitions to become an industrial outlet. In the middle of the nineteenth century there were plans to develop iron ore production in the Barle valley and along the northern rim of Exmoor. A bed was laid for a railway line to transport the ore to the coast, but preliminary work in the mines failed to reveal sufficiently extensive veins to justify large-scale investment. There were some bitter financial disputes: the project was dropped, the lines were never laid, and Porlock Weir stayed the way it was. Porlock itself, a short step inland, is famous for two things: its terrifyingly steep hill, and the Person who one day walked to Culbone to drop in for a chat with Samuel Taylor Coleridge, arriving in time to interrupt his transcription of a fantastic dream he had had under the influence of opium, and so robbing us of all save a fragment of *Kubla Khan*.

Dunster in Somerset was once a harbour of fair importance, but was robbed of this distinction when the river mouth silted up. It remains faithful to the sea, however, providing sailors with a sturdy seamark in the shape of the Conygar Hill Tower. At the other end of the village street is a Norman castle which in a thousand years has been in the possession of only two families. During the Civil War it was attacked first by the Royalists and then by Parliament, and during the later phases of the struggle was the only place in Somerset still to fly the royal standard. The *Luttrell Arms* inn takes its name from the castellans of the last six centuries, and there are Luttrell monuments in the church. Among the village's other treasures are a dovecote complete with its original revolving ladder, a slate-hung medieval nunnery, a yarn cross with wide overhanging eaves and eight gabled windows which has been here since the early seventeenth century, the truncated pillar of an old butter cross, and over the River Avill a pack-horse bridge.

Turning back to Land's End to start exploring the southern coast, we are back in the land of the pilchard fishers. Only now there are no pilchards, and the remaining boats in the old harbours are more commonly used for taking visitors around the bays, or occasionally taking the more adventurous out shark-fishing.

For hundreds of years the pilchard catches meant almost as much to Cornwall as its tin mining profits. Every village had its 'huer' watching from the cliff-tops for the tell-tale glow beneath the surface of the sea which indicated the arrival of a shoal, so that the cry of 'Heva, heva!' could send the boats racing out with their seines; and every village had its courtyard houses with fish 'cellars' for curing and storing the catch. At first the fish were stacked up in layers pressed upon alternating layers of salt, but in later years of the trade they were immersed in salt vats for several weeks. There were times when a season's catch could amount to fifty thousand hogsheads, and over a hundred million pilchards were exported in one fruitful year. Then an increase in foreign export duties, plus the removal of a Government subsidy at home, hit the trade hard. The fishermen struggled on, and in this century canneries were built at Mevagissey and other small ports. But by now there was another snag: the pilchards just weren't returning to their old areas. Drifters had to go out looking for them further afield; and soon even this proved an unrewarding business.

Jack Pender, whose paintings of harbours and boats are known far beyond his native Mousehole, tries in his work to preserve the essential qualities of the village as he knew it in his boyhood, before it is too late. Away during the Second World War and later at art school, he was shocked by the changes he found on his return—changes which continue at an increasing pace. Living in a house perched on the edge of the harbour he turns again and again to the harbour walls and the crane on the quay as subjects, and even more obsessively to craft drawn up on the shore or setting out to sea. Capturing the essence of a boat and its background is no simple matter, for a boat is different to different people: to the holidaymaker fancying 'a day in the sun on a smooth sea', a weekend fisherman wanting little more than to potter about, or to the fisherman whose livelihood it represents, and therefore represents work, money and worry.

A guidebook published in the early 1950s and reprinted not so long ago refers to 'the pilchard fishing fleet' in Mousehole harbour. At the time of writing there is only one first-class boat operating in the old family tradition—and even then, the two brothers working it have to commute to Newlyn to carry on most of their business.

Tin mining, too, fell on hard times long ago. Its chimney-stacks and engine-houses have become ruins almost as picturesque as those of ancient castles. Indeed, the industry is more ancient than many a cherished Ancient Monument. Rising out of the bay near the clustered houses and palm trees of Marazion, St Michael's Mount claims to be the last visible fragment of lost Lyonesse, in which the 'last great battle of the West' was fought and Arthur came to his final confrontation with Modred. But the mount was an island many centuries before Arthur's supposed lifetime. In about 325 B.C. the Greek explorer Pytheas visited Britain and recorded how tin was mined and smelted, and also how at low tide it was carried to the islet of Ictis for sale to Continental traders. There can be little doubt that St Michael's Mount is that same Ictis, still joined to Marazion by a causeway at low tide.

Another, more substantial rock tacked on to the mainland is that of the Isle of Portland. The link is formed by the shingle wall of Chesil Bank, today sheltering an approach road which joins the great limestone outcrop at Chesilton. Before the road was laid, people and horses had at most times of day to cross by ferry. Not that traffic was all that brisk: although the Romans quarried the stone from time to time, the island was never a hospitable place and did not encourage settlers—but once folk *had* settled, they cut themselves off almost wilfully from the mainlanders. 'Be 'e one o' we?' is a question still asked when an unfamiliar face appears in the village street. For a long time administration was carried on in a purely local, distinctive way. If any land deal was projected, both vendor and purchaser had to make a declaration in church of the proposed transaction, which was then regarded as legally settled. The church or the local inn would keep records of land holdings by means of 'reed poles' into which notches were cut to show every man's acreage.

With a shortage of fresh water, villages of necessity grew up around such wells as could be found, and were often named after them: Fortuneswell, for example, and Southwell. Portland stone is so hard that until the invention of adequate machinery it was difficult to cut it into manageable blocks. The houses and cottages of the steep village streets are impossible to date at a glance: heavy and chunky, with little variation in the sombre off-white stone, they are as much a part of an eternal landscape as are the granite churches of Cornwall. Fortuneswell church here was built by convicts from the grim prison, now a Borstal; Southwell church from donations made by the friends and relations of those killed when two ships collided. Over churches, cottages, roofs, doorsteps, streets and dismal grass lies everywhere a fine, inescapable, gritty dust. A visitor peering into the vast chasm of one of the quarries once said: 'You could put St Paul's Cathedral in there.' To which came the justifiable reply: 'St Paul's Cathedral came *out* of there.'

By the time we reach the Hampshire coast we are in a world of dinghy sailors, of speedboats, of creeks and inlets with expensive club-houses, and villages which are nearly all in danger of being engulfed by some spreading holiday resort. Some still cling to proud memories. Buckler's Hard, tucked away up the River Beaulieu, stands delightfully between water and forest. Oak from the New Forest supplied its eighteenth-century shipyards, from which many of the vessels destined for Nelson's fleet were towed to Portsmouth for fitting out. Nelson's own *Agamemnon* was built here. These great days are recalled in the little maritime museum opened by Earl Mountbatten in 1963, and in the remarkable width of the main street, laid out to provide space for the stacking and weathering of timber.

The inlets of Chichester Harbour similarly have their forests of masts, and inn signs sporting jolly sailors, anchors and spread sails. The few remaining eighteenth-century cottages of Itchenor are lost in a bright expansion of Italianate, Scandinavian and Toyland bungalows, with plenty of garden space and some palatial garages. It remains easy on the eye, but hard on the pocket of any prospective settler.

Bosham has acquired many similar additions, but remains delightful. One feels oneself in the presence of history and at the same time of a living village. In pagan times a courageous Celtic monk, Dicul, lived here in a cell which is thought to be in the crypt beneath the present church, and prayed here with a group of fellow believers before St Wilfrid ever set foot in Sussex to found his diocese of Selsey. Quay Meadow, a stretch of greensward between the lovely Saxon watch-tower of the church and the creek, is one of the contenders for the distinction of being the spot where King Canute ordered the waves to retreat. Certainly Canute was responsible for much of the existing church, including the nave, and the story that his eight-year-old daughter was buried here, at one time derided by sceptics, received some support when a stone coffin containing the remains of just such a child was uncovered in 1865, and moved again during restorations in 1954. A memorial plaque in Royal Copenhagen porcelain has been installed, bearing Canute's emblem of the black raven.

At low tide it is possible to drive along a track beside the flats on which boats lie high and dry—or perhaps high and a bit damp. It is inadvisable to park and go away, however. When the tide comes in, it thrusts right up against the walls of the village, and traffic signs and road markings offer incongruous directions across the watery surface.

The shipwrights of the south coast often built shacks, boat-houses and dwellings for themselves, and found it simpler to do so by employing the skills with which they were most familiar. To keep the salt rain and spray out, they covered their houses with planking treated with pitch and caulked as in a boat. The habit spread. Where wood was plentiful, either from local plantations or imported from Scandinavia, the technique of weather-boarding ('clapboard' in America) developed. Lead oxide was substituted for pitch, and all across Sussex and Kent sprang up the white-painted weather-boarded houses, windmills and watermills which still brighten hilltops, riverside tracks and village streets. Sometimes this cheap but attractive method was used to re-face older houses, giving a misleading appearance: I know of one small Sussex house which throughout my childhood carried weather-boarding, only to reveal years later that behind this façade was some impressive half-timbering. But even the half-timbering was not altogether authentic: it masked earlier, much nobler brickwork.

One of the most striking timbered smock mills, both landmark and seamark, stands on the slopes above Rottingdean. Built early in the eighteenth century, it was moved to its present position in 1802. The last practising miller lived in a house still called Mill Cottage in the village High Street. But grinding corn was at times only a subsidiary function: the mill played a key part in Rottingdean's most profitable trade, conveying messages and urgent warnings to smugglers by the set of its sails.

The coast in this region is an abomination of villas and vulgarity, but a few yards behind the clamorous main road the village of Rottingdean preserves its cobbled cottages, a *Black Horse* inn whose lounge was once the village smithy, and around the green and pond the one-time homes of Kipling, Burne-Jones, William Nicholson and other writers and artists. Whipping Post House was for some years the home of Captain Dunk, a famous local smuggler; and in the church an impressive bust commemorates Thomas Hooker, vicar between 1792 and 1838, among whose ways of serving his parishioners was that of acting as look-out when contraband cargoes were being run ashore and hidden in the cliff face or in the web of subterranean passages still to be traced beneath the village street. It was probably from local reminiscences that Kipling derived inspiration for his poem recommending insomniacs to watch the wall while the Gentlemen go by, and promising brandy for the parson.

Clerics, beside the sea or further inland, seem to have been very amenable to persuasion from the free traders. The most famous or infamous gangs often operated from headquarters deep in the country, shifting their booty from coastal hideouts to rural graveyards and church towers or roofs. Pirate turned clergyman, clergyman turned smuggler—the rôle must be derived by novelists, poets and playwrights from an amalgam of real-life characters in this part of England. J. M. Barrie based his Captain Hook on stories he was told of such a man in Brede, a village set above a river which winds down to Pett Level to flank the territory of the powerful Romney Marsh smugglers. It may be that from this same source Russell Thorndike derived Doctor Syn. The smugglers hurrying their loads along the secret lanes and valleys of this region had their own cause to be grateful to Brede and its medieval manor house. Begun in 1350, it was greatly extended two hundred years later by the Oxenbridge family. Abandoned and decrepit in later years, it became a rendez-vous for smugglers and provided a useful cache for their booty. It was they who must have boosted up the old legends about Sir Goddard Oxenbridge so that local inhabitants would believe it was haunted and shun it, especially if strange lights were seen and inexplicable noises heard. Sir Goddard was reputed to be a giant who could not go to bed until he had supped on a child or two. He met his death when the children of Sussex rebelled and, catching him unawares, sawed him in two. Thereafter he haunted the Groaning Bridge over the stream, and paced through the corridors of Brede Place. One disconcerting fact is that, long after the place had ceased to be of use to smugglers—and long after bricklayers repairing the house broke into an unsuspected chamber containing hoarded jewel-lery—the presence of the ghost was confirmed by owners and visitors with no devious reasons for scaring the locals. Stephen Crane, author of *The Red Badge of Courage*, had several odd experiences while he was renting the house; and the sculptress Clare Sheridan, some of whose work can be seen in Brede church, recounts some of her own bewilderments in *My Crowded Sanctuary*.

In Essex, Suffolk and Norfolk too there were well-known landing places such as the hamlet of Sizewell (now the site of an atomic power station) and the sandhills around Winterton, and efficient routes to distribution centres. St Andrew's church at Westhall, down a winding lane in a secluded corner of East Suffolk, has a double roof with a gully invisible from ground level, reached by ladders which some thatcher or other local workman could be relied on to leave within easy reach.

By the time we reach these East Anglian shores we are far, in every way, from the defiant granite of Land's End. Attacked by the North Sea, these low sandy cliffs surrender time after time, retreat year after year. Dunwich, once the most important city on this coast, is now only a village with a couple of smokehouses, a pub, a tiny museum, and the crumbling shell of a priory. Shipden, near Cromer, and Slaughden, once a fishing village of more consequence than neighbouring Aldeburgh, are now at the bottom of the sea. Those who choose to live here have always been prepared to face not only the scour of the water but also the lash of an unrelenting east wind. Strangely, there is nothing bleak in the architecture of the coastal villages themselves: white and bright, pink-washed and pargeted, with tall church towers like beacons for passing seamen, they somehow convey good cheer in the worst of weathers. 'If you can stick it for six months,' newcomers are told, 'you'll live for ever.' Not so long ago it was said of an old lady hereabouts: 'I think she's ninety-seven, but she's been over ninety for so long, I've lost track.'

The smugglers are still with us. The little villages of the Orwell and Deben estuaries and the shaded upper reaches of the rivers are associated with Margaret Catchpole, born in 1773 and drawn into desperate deeds by her smuggling lover, Will Laud: Levington creek, below the snug, low-ceilinged *Ship* inn; the Cat House at Woolverstone, where a white cat was set in the window to give the 'all clear' for a landing; Ramsholt and Waldringfield with their little sailing communities, not so many miles from the dockside clamours of Ipswich and Felixstowe yet quite sheltered from them; and Pin Mill, whose *Butt and Oyster* inn has one of the finest views in the country, out over glistening flats at low tide, over water coming right up to its wall at high tide, with some of the last great sailing barges laid up a few yards from the bar window.

The rector of Great Bealings in the first decades of the nineteenth century was thoughtful enough to leave his stable unlocked when he heard that smugglers would be at work in the Deben and up Martlesham Creek that night. They would use his coach, well known in the district and unlikely to be discourteously stopped by Preventive officers, and return it in the small hours together with some additional item of luggage as a thank-offering. Parson Woodforde's diary of his Norfolk incumbency nowhere suggests that he rendered such active assistance to Norfolk counterparts, but he was a regular and unashamed customer. One senses his relief in the entry:

> John Buck, the blacksmith, who was lately informed against for having a Tub of Gin found in his House that was smuggled, by two Excise Officers, was pretty easy fined.

At Blakeney, news of the imminent arrival of an illicit cargo would bring out every man who owned a horse and cart, eager to help and to collect the fees which the smugglers gladly paid. They boasted that Preventive men rarely caught up with them because they had been effectively bribed not to do so—'And we always left a keg just inside the parson's gate.'

Blakeney was once a prosperous little port, closer to the sea than it is now. Silting of the Glaven estuary has left it with only a winding approach creek, but its quayside is still bright and active—with weekend sailors and holidaymakers. Shortly before the Second World War many of the fishermen's cottages were no more than hovels. Today the place has become a smartly painted, renovated, fashionable little retreat. Its steep, narrow main street gives it the air of a Cornish village, though it has not yet been banned to traffic. On a wall facing out to the distant sea is a mark showing the level which that sea reached when, in 1953, it raged back and devastatingly flooded this whole coastline.

The estuary is guarded—none too well in 1953—by the shallow arm of Blakeney Point, a nature reserve which extends five miles from its extreme tip eastwards to Cley-next-the-Sea. Cley isn't next-the-sea, either, though it has one fairly short, solid road to the actual shore. Like Blakeney, it once prospered when the Glaven estuary was open; and, like Blakeney, has shrunk to village size. Its streets twist between flinty houses as if to ensure that the wind never finds any straight channel to blow down, and thrusting up against that wind is a sturdy red-brick windmill dating from 1713. The façade of the post office merits attention: its peculiar texture is due to the grinding together of bones and teeth of horses and cattle.

This coast has not been entirely the preserve of smugglers. In the little cluster of Burnham parishes, Horatio Nelson was born in 1758 in Burnham Thorpe's parsonage, now demolished but recalled by a

8   *Arlington Row, Bibury, Gloucestershire*

roadside plaque. The church also contains many Nelson and other naval mementoes. Another defier of the nation's enemies is the village of Weybourne, where it was long ago declared:

> *He who would old England win*
> *Must at Weybourne Hope begin.*

Weybourne Hope is the name of the shingly beach below the cliffs, shelving so steeply that ships of considerable draught can get close inshore. Fortunately there was no Norfolk fifth-columnist to leak this information to Adolf Hitler; or if there was, the Führer failed to pay sufficient heed.

One remembers, too, the Polish seaman who became Joseph Conrad, an English novelist. He spoke of the North Sea as his schoolroom, his teachers being

> the sailors of the Norfolk shore; coast men, with steady eyes, mighty limbs, and gentle voice ... each built as though to last forever ... gold hair and blue eyes with that Northern straight-away-there look!

The further we go up this coast, along the flat rim of Lincolnshire towards the rising cliffs and craggier rocks of Yorkshire, Durham and Northumberland, the more often we find that the wind which Lincolnshire resorts doggedly assure the tourist is 'so bracing' is damped down by something known as a 'sea fret'. From wartime and later experience in Whitley Bay, Cullercoats and other such places, I can vouch for this being a euphemism for a bitter, clinging, choking white fog differing from the old London pea-souper only in colour. It can make the greyer stone villages eerie and, on the surface, inhospitable. But none of them is inhospitable; and not all of them are grey.

Robin Hood's Bay, prodded in piece by piece like an eccentric three-dimensional jigsaw which the sagging gap in the cliffs north of Ravenscar threatens to shake off as jumbled fragments into the sea, is an unexpected glow of red-tiled roofs above brown, grey and golden stone, brick, and occasional splashes of white surfacing and colour washes. The houses are tightly packed at a dizzying variety of angles and elevations. Associations with Robin Hood are tenuous. One story has it that Robin of Barnesdale frequently preyed on rich prelates and their followers going to and from Whitby Abbey, and established useful contacts with local fishermen. Boats were kept ready for them in the bay against possible emergency, and when enemies did begin to close in on the outlaws they made use of these to get away.

Some prehistoric barrows on the moor above are known as Robin Hood Butts. One wonders if future generations will find appropriate nicknames for the nearby globes of Fylingdales Early Warning Station.

Runswick Bay, too, has its houses crammed in on steep slopes and into twists and gaps in the rock behind the headland. Its sea wall is like some chipped and eroded military defence work. When the fishing boats set sail it used to be the custom to sacrifice a cat in hope of a safe return; but, pessimistic about the efficacy of this, local wives also developed the most complicated patterns in the guernseys they knitted for their menfolk—not as an artistic exercise, but so that corpses washed ashore after long submersion could be identified. There were other odd customs here. It was believed that whooping-cough could be cured by the hobs or brownies, and any child so afflicted was hurried to a cave in the bay, still known as Hob Hole, where the parents would intone:

> Hob-hole Hob,
> My bairn's gotten kink cough.
> Tak't off, tak't off!

Staithes makes use of yet another bay, approached by a gradient almost as alarming as the notorious one at Porlock. The name of the village means simply a landing-place, common in both Norse and Old English and found frequently added to places in the Fens and on the Broads. The harbour prospered from the cod and haddock trade, but this was gradually weaned away by busier Whitby. James Cook was apprenticed at the age of twelve to a haberdasher here, but after an argument with his employer went off to sea as a collier's apprentice and later fame as a marine surveyor.

It is difficult to keep one's temper when writing about the Durham coast, dominated, as the authors of the *Good Beach Guide* rightly observe, by the National Coal Board. Generations of feckless profiteers and equally irresponsible government-appointed managers have disposed of waste from the conglomeration of coal mines by tipping it into the sea and along the sand. Seaham must have been a remote little village when Lord Byron married Anne Isabella Milbanke at a private ceremony in Seaham Hall, now a hospital. It has a Saxon church with later additions, including a Jacobean pulpit and an impressive array of box pews. But all is overshadowed by the industrialization which took over when, thirteen years after Byron's ill-starred marriage, the Marquess of Londonderry founded Seaham Harbour to cope with the output of the nearby coalfield.

The black horror of it all shades away towards Whitburn, which retains a trim little village green and a church spire long trusted as a seamark on this stretch of coast. And at last there is one unpolluted stretch of shore and cliffs about Marsden Bay, looking out to the freakish arch of Marsden Rock through which small boats can make their way if their owners are not too scared of the droppings of raucous resident kittiwakes and cormorants.

Northumberland has never allowed itself to be subjugated by industry or by much else. Once past the high presbytery ruins of Tynemouth priory on the north bank of the busy river, we find few unsightly stretches and indeed few townships or inlets of any size. The stark little fishing villages have no deep-cut coves to protect them, but man-made defences have been attempted at various times to encourage the fishing trade or provide facilities for coal and lime coasters. Minor trading posts such as Alnmouth, Boulmer and Beadnell, and Craster with its houses of disconcertingly massive slabs of basaltic stone, have become the regular holiday resorts of discerning adherents who return year after year, fiercely partisan and oblivious to the lack of fairgrounds and amusement arcades.

Bamburgh is altogether a different, and more ancient, matter. Here the Angles established their first major settlement in 547. It became the capital of Northumbria, and after the Norman Conquest the site of a royal castle. The keep which Henry II perched on an outcrop of the Whin Sill escarpment, and later additions to the castle, had to be constructed from stone brought in by sea: quarrying and cutting the iron-hard dolerite, close to hand as it might be, was too arduous a business. Today the village, part of the Crewe Estate, looks feudally respectful around its triangular green below that imposing headland. Its church of St Aidan recalls long associations with the monastery of Aidan and Cuthbert on Lindisfarne.

The first real lifeboat station in Britain and perhaps in the world came into being here late in the eighteenth century with help from the Crewe Trust, and in 1824 the Royal National Lifeboat Institution was formed to co-ordinate rescue operations all along our coasts. It took a long time to establish a comprehensive service. Harbours of all sizes had their own methods in time of emergency: local men would put out in their own boats to rescue the drowning, or would support a boat designed specifically for the purpose. In some periods of history—not so very long ago, at that—rescue boats were maintained only by the money which could be claimed for salvage, and it was not unknown for neighbouring villages to send out rival boats and fight for the right to be first aboard a wreck. 'East coast pirates' is a term of jovial abuse still used by many North Sea fishermen and life-boat men of their predecessors and the sons and grandsons of those predecessors.

Even with the R.N.L.I. established and in operation, individual bravery still counted for as much as rational organization. When the steamship *Forfarshire* went aground on the Farne islands during a gale in September 1838, it was not the Bamburgh station which went into action but a girl in her early twenties, whose name is preserved on a gravestone in St Aidan's churchyard and in Bamburgh's little museum. Grace Darling and her father, keeper of the Longstone lighthouse, rowed their own coble through turbulent seas to where nine survivors of the wreck were clinging to the rocks. It took two trips to get all nine safely back to the lighthouse. From inquiries into the disaster, and a welter of recriminations, the girl emerged as the heroine of the hour. Sadly she lived to enjoy her fame for only another four years, but symbolically she was to prove of undying worth to the more intensive development of the lifeboat service.

Rowing boats and sailing boats were replaced by steam-driven and then by oil-driven craft. In some areas larger boats have been withdrawn to make way for smaller, faster inshore rescue boats where holiday sailors and swimmers constitute a more frequent risk of alarm calls than do large-scale wrecks. Sometimes large and small vessels work from the same base. It might be thought that the withdrawal from a small community of any lifeboat whatsoever would be a relief to wives and even to the men themselves: if a stretch of coast can be adequately covered by more modern craft from near-by, larger places, then surely one-time crew members can sleep more soundly and be assured of a longer life? In fact, local pride is always hurt when a station closes down. In 1856 the Suffolk village of Kessingland was supplied with its first official lifeboat, and in January of the following year saved the crew of a schooner which foundered. By 1884 conditions along this treacherous coast were so bad that Kessingland acquired two more boats, and operated all three for the next fifteen years. As late as the 1930s the station was still using a sailing boat, and it was decided that this could be eliminated by the introduction of longer-range motor boats from stations to either side of the village. In 1936 the station closed down. The last recognizable shreds of the life-boat shed are incorporated into a small amusement arcade. As for Caister, north of Yarmouth, when the R.N.L.I. decided there was no need to continue with its services a few years ago, the local people raised funds to buy and maintain their own boat, and maintain their great tradition.

It was a retired Caister coxswain who uttered one of the most famous declarations in lifeboat history, after two of his sons, two grandsons and a son-in-law were lost in a capsize: 'Caister men never turn back'. There are villages, still, which put a high proportion of their breadwinners at risk whenever the boat is launched. Hardly a family in little Rye Harbour was unscathed by the loss of seventeen men in November 1928 when the *Mary Stanford* was turned over in a south-westerly gale. In spite of modern improvements, the sea still has terrible reserves of destructive strength. Having taken five people off a fishing boat in distress, the Seaham lifeboat capsized in November 1962 with the loss of the whole crew and four of the rescued men. Self-righting boats are coming increasingly into use; but storm and currents and jagged rocks or insidious sandbanks will always offer cruel, unpredictable hazards and make a mockery of men's handiwork—but not of their courage.

Across the narrowing neck of the country, St Bees on the Cumbrian coast has one of the faster inshore vessels to watch over its increasing influx of holidaymakers, who seem to have discovered the place only about twenty years ago. It has been there a long time. Its Saxon church was destroyed by the Norsemen, and St Bega is believed to have founded a Benedictine nunnery here: the church is dedicated to SS Mary and Bega. A sixteenth-century Archbishop of Canterbury, son of the village, founded the grammar school which has now become a public school.

Some of these Irish Sea and Morecambe Bay villages seem positively complacent after the wind-bitten hamlets and nesses of the east. Barrow-in-Furness may darken the skies, but the coal pits of Maryport no longer tip their slag on the foreshore, and the authorities of County Durham might well emulate the policies here, where derelict tracts disfigured by past industry are being cleaned up to provide new recreational facilities. In many places the sea recedes so far at low tide, and sometimes stays away for so long, that the inhabitants might justifiably feel they had been deserted. Across great tracts of Morecambe Bay the shrimpers have to drive out with tractors if they are to organize and collect their catch—maritime farmers ranging out from their smallholdings, rather than fishermen. But when the water does come back it can do so swiftly and murderously, cutting off what appeared to be safe and golden sand— and, if it is in the mood, flooding roads in the Heysham area. The trim little village of Stalmine, with its old village green where there used to be fairs and bull-baiting, was in danger of complete inundation in the middle of the eighteenth century.

In the tripartite estuary of the Esk, the Mite and the Irt, Ravenglass has happily abandoned pretensions to being a busy port and settled for fishing and tourism. It was once the terminal of a narrow-gauge mineral railway, now running a passenger service throughout the year, much extended for summer traffic. Just outside the village are

remains of the Roman fort of Glannaventa, and between this and Mun-
caster Castle have been found evidence of a Roman tile works. The
castle itself has fine gardens and a treasured cup presented by Henry
VI, brought in from the fells by shepherds and given shelter after
the battle of Hexham during the Wars of the Roses. Tradition has it
that the family prosperity will remain unbroken so long as the cup
is unbroken.

Silverdale, where Mrs Gaskell lived for a time at Lindeth Tower
and which retains the Gaskell Institute, sits in a region of natural
beauty, with long walks over the limestone knotts, commanding
wide views of the saltings and Morecambe Bay, much of it such as
Castlebarrow and Arnside Knott protected by the National Trust.
Morecambe and Heysham were once villages, but have flowed together into a small-scale Blackpool.

Further south, Overton and Glasson face each other across the
mouth of the Lune. Overton is linked to the once busy Sunderland
Point by a causeway whose safe negotiation, like the deceptively
open sands, requires knowledge of the tricks of the tide. Its fishermen's cottages and shops, and its old inn, have their counterparts
in Glasson, though that may just possibly be in a precarious balance
between one industrial period and another. Glasson outstripped
Sunderland Point as a harbour serving Lancaster, and was once a
bustle of Scandinavian and Canadian timber boats. It has now
slowed the pace and is an agreeable little marina for weekend relaxa-
tion; but new industrial complexes are beginning to edge in on it.

Coastal villages are, in effect, perpetually threatened by erosion
both from the sea and from the land; by a trading prosperity which
robs them of the charm which might bring visitors to see them—
and by brash and thoughtless visitors who ruin the very aspects of
the place which they have come so far to see.

CHAPTER THREE

The West Country

Although we associate the western extremity of the country with greyness and granite, outside of the Land's End promontory this rock in fact occurs only as pockets in much larger beds of sandstone. On and around the moors are chunky, leaden villages; but there are just as many in mellow red-gold stone—and nothing could look warmer than the cottages of the sun-blest South Hams among their near-tropical vegetation.

Scattered blocks of surface moorstone are found inserted into farmhouse walls, bridges and churches, and quarries such as Bosinjack and Trenowath still supply granite for pavements and building stone. There are many slate quarries, including those near Ashburton in Devon which provide the many greeny-brown roofs of the region. Beer used to produce a complete contrast in its hard grey-white limestone. And the whole scene turns a deeper gold as we move up towards the softer limestone of the Cotswolds.

There were never any extensive forests beyond the Tamar, so timber constructions in Cornwall were rare. The simpler houses here and in Devon were usually built of cob, a compressed mixture of mud and slate chippings set on a shallow pebbled base and thatched. Bricks did not make any significant contribution until the early eighteenth century.

Quarrying, tin mining, crawling into fogous: the Cornishmen seem to have spent much of their time digging a way into the ground. Specimens of the early steam engines used for draining their subterranean workings, known as Cornish Engines, are preserved and can be inspected by arrangement at Camborne and St Just mines; and, worthily enough, Trevithick's birthplace at Camborne is also looked after by the National Trust. Near Madron, whose granite church of St Madernus is the mother church of Penzance, is the abandoned Ding Dong tin mine. Older religions are also remembered in granite, in burial barrows such as Lanyon Quoit a couple of miles out of the village.

To the west, a little way beyond Marazion, Goldsithney has an unusual museum of mechanical musical instruments, predecessors of those electronic synthesizers which may soon, we hope, lapse to the same level of mere curiosity value. Along the same road there is a complete contrast at Godolphin Cross, where the Tudor mansion which was the ancestral home of the Godolphins is open to the public, displaying some impressive colonnades of local granite installed early in the seventeenth century.

The names of villages such as St Just-in-Roseland and St Anthony-in-Roseland conjure up delectable visions of a flower-bedecked landscape. Luxuriant as many of the cottage gardens are, the description means very much the opposite: it comes from a Cornish word *ros*, meaning heathland. Adding another linguistic twist, Veryan-in-Roseland is a corruption of the name of St Symphorian, whose village church has a staunch little platoon of devout supporters: a Regency eccentric built five circular thatched cottages each topped with a cross, theorizing that since the Devil is known to conceal himself in corners he could best be thwarted by round dwellings with no such corners.

We have already followed the indented, once harsh but now almost over-sociable coastline. The truer faces of the Western Men and their world can perhaps be better seen on and about the moors which rise and are tamed, only to emerge again, across country from Bodmin Moor through Dartmoor, Exmoor and Sedgemoor to fabled 'Egdon Heath' and Salisbury Plain.

High on Bodmin Moor is the insignificant little hamlet of Bolventor overshadowed by its notorious inn. Everything about this old coaching inn is out of scale with its humble neighbours: wide cobbled courtyard, wide granite fireplace, and oak supports as mighty as tree trunks. Outside, the sign of *Jamaica Inn* dramatically echoes the mood of Daphne du Maurier's novel. Inside, where some pubs go in for horse-brasses and warming-pans, this one features smugglers' lanterns, pistols and brandy casks. A revenant who haunts the surrounding wastes is said to be Jan Tregeagle, a corrupt seventeenth-century magistrate buried in an unmarked grave in St Breoc churchyard but not allowed to rest there for long. One of the phantom tasks he is doomed to carry out in punishment for his misdeeds is the emptying of Dozmary Pool, a mile and a half south of Bolventor, with a limpet shell riddled with holes. Since the pool is supposedly bottomless, this task ought to keep him busy for eternity. In fact the pool has been known to dry up in times of drought, which rather spoils another legend: it is also supposed to be the lake into which Sir Bedivere threw Excalibur, but nobody yet has found Arthur's sword on the dry bottom.

On the way to Dartmoor we find Devon full of Bucklands. There are Buckland Brew near Bideford, and Buckland Filleigh near Black Torrington; Buckland Tout Saints and West Buckland, and more besides. Buckland Monachorum is 'of the monks' by reason of Buckland Abbey, a thirteenth-century Cistercian foundation. After the Dissolution it became the home first of Sir Richard Grenville, whose grandson—commander of the *Revenge*—made extensive alterations, adding a plaster ceiling and friezes to the great hall. In 1581 it was bought by Sir Francis Drake on his triumphal return from circumnavigating the world, and has now become a museum containing Drake's drum together with portraits and relics of both Grenville and Drake.

Above the River Dart, Buckland-in-the-Moor is, as its name implies, well into Dartmoor; but it is sheltered and enriched by beech woods, and its granite softened by thatched roofs. The face of the church clock has letters instead of numerals, spelling out MY DEAR MOTHER.

Also 'in-the-Moor', literally *in* it, in a protective cleft, is Widecombe. Known as 'cathedral of the moor', the church of St Pancras has a tall granite tower which was struck by lightning in 1638, when some of the villagers were killed. Near by, the fifteenth-century Church House is partly a cottage, partly the village hall. Remote and self-sufficient, Widecombe is one of those places which gain immortal fame from some fluke—in this case the song telling of Uncle Tom Cobleigh and his friends on their way to Widecombe Fair. This is pictured in the village sign, and is still held annually in September.

Still deeper into—or on to—the moor, we come to Postbridge, a hamlet with one of the stone clapper bridges across which drovers urged their sheep and cattle in the Middle Ages, and merchants drove packhorses laden with the output of the mines. Much older relics are those of the prehistoric pounds, of which more than a hundred have been identified: the largest, Broadun Pound, had a wall enclosing twelve acres, within which sheep and cattle would be penned and a number of huts built.

On the northern fringe of Dartmoor is Sampford Courtenay, whose granite church is leavened with polyphant, a dark blue-green, marble-like stone from quarries near the Cornish hamlet of Polyphant. The rest of the village is largely Devon cob, colour washed and topped with thatch, with some red sandstone. It is a tranquil corner; yet from here spread, in 1549, a violent revolt which fired the country and was suppressed only by even more violent measures.

The Western Rebellion, or Devonshire Rebellion, was sparked off by the Act of Uniformity commanding the clergy to accept and use Cranmer's vernacular Book of Common Prayer on and from Whit Sunday, 1549. Many clerics and many congregations objected. In Sampford Courtenay the objections were so forceful that the next day the priest was made to start all over again with Mass in the old style. Other churches followed suit. Religious protest was turned into pitched battles, in which foreign mercenaries were brought in to slaughter the peasants. Final defeat of the objectors was accomplished at Sampford Courtenay, where it had all begun. Hundreds of those who survived the sword were hanged for treason.

Some way to the east, almost into Exeter, is another clean-scrubbed, thatched village built to a less haphazard pattern than many. Newton St Cyres was probably planned, suggests Professor Pevsner, by an eighteenth-century lord of the manor. Its church is dedicated to St Cyricus and St Julitta, a mother and three-year-old son martyred by Diocletian. The only other church in Britain with these patrons is to be found at Swaffham Prior in Cambridgeshire. On the Northcote family memorial are plaques of the heads of two wives, with a record of their achievements or lack of same.

The first declares:

> *My fruite was small*
> *One sonne was all*
> *That not at all.*

And the second:

> *My Jacob had by mee*
> *As many sons as hee*
> *Daughters twice three.*

In a county so famous for its seafaring men, it is fitting that along-side the embowered hamlet of Arlington near the western rim of Exmoor we should find Arlington Court, owned by the Chichester family from the fourteenth century until our own times. Their most celebrated descendant in this century was the yachtsman, Sir Francis Chichester. The present house was built early in the 1800s and contains, among other collections, one of model ships. The River Yeo runs right through the landscaped grounds, accompanied by an attractive walk.

When we set foot on Exmoor we inevitably begin, as most visitors do, searching for authentic traces of the fictitious Doones. But were they purely fictional? The author admitted that he had shifted the scenery about a bit to suit the dictates of his story, but insisted that the characters in *Lorna Doone* were based on fact. There does seem to be reliable evidence of a gang of outlaws settling early in the seventeenth century in the ruined long-houses of Badgworthy, a Saxon village which continued to flourish into the twelfth century and whose remaining fragments are now known irrevocably as the Doones' houses. These outcasts lived by robbing and murdering travellers and by raiding isolated farms. Their brutality became so outrageous that the locals eventually combined to attack their bleak settlement and drive them out. The name of Doone may come from a mistaken identification with earlier Danish raiders, or from Scottish exiles from Doune who settled in the Oare valley. Other theories make them Royalists left destitute after the Roundhead victories. Oare church rests secure in its claim to be the scene of Lorna's wedding, and according to R. D. Blackmore's novel it was through a window on the south side of the chancel that Carver Doone shot her. A portrait medallion was put up in 1925 to commemorate the centenary of the author's birth.

The highest hamlet in Exmoor, with its church tower thrusting up from a fold in the ground, is Stoke Pero, one of the earliest known Christian settlements on the moor. No more than a scattering of farmsteads, its loneliness has been linked in an old jingle with that of two other none too easily accessible places:

> *Culbone, Oare and Stoke Pero,*
> *Parishes three, no parson'll go.*

But parsons did go. One in the fourteenth century is tantalizingly on record as having carried off the wife of one of his parishioners.

The Quantocks are geologically an outrider of Exmoor. Beyond them we come to the levels and mysteries of Sedgemoor—of Glastonbury, its tor and its thorn, and of the elusive Arthur once more. Outside West Pennard a stone marks the site of the Pontis Vallum, a fort guarding the bridge which linked the Isle of Avalon to 'the mainland'. A hummock by East Lyng bears a stone in honour of King Alfred's stay on the Isle of Athelney while preparing his comeback against the Danes. And Weston Zoyland stands close to the spot where the last major battle on English soil was fought.

The Church Tower of Weston Zoyland, visible for miles around, was raised by an abbot of Glastonbury. The interior has a superbly carved nave roof. Into the church came many of the dead and wounded from the brief engagement in 1685 which put paid to the Duke of Monmouth's hopes. Some of James II's soldiers were buried in the churchyard, others in the church itself. Of the wounded rebels, many were slain on the spot, some died of wounds, and others had to await the bloody mercies of Judge Jeffreys.

To the north rises the carboniferous limestone ridge of the Mendips. There are few settlements on the plateau itself, but villages nestle on the lower slopes and in the openings of dried-up valleys. Caves have been gouged out by underground rivers, the most famous being those in Cheddar Gorge. The village of Cheddar has an old market cross and remnants of a Saxon royal palace; and a museum of old cars to complement the thousands of modern cars which choke the gorge. Defoe describes the scene two hundred and fifty years ago:

> Before the village is a large green, or common, a piece of ground in which the whole herd of the cows belonging to the town do feed; the ground is exceeding rich, and as the whole village are cowkeepers, they take care to keep up the goodness of the soil by agreeing to lay on large quantities of dung for manuring and enriching the land. The milk of all the town cows, is brought together every day in a common room, where the persons appointed, or trusted for the management, measure every man's quantity, and set it down in a book; when the quantities are adjusted, the milk is all put together, and every meal's milk makes one cheese, and no more; so that the cheese is bigger, or less, as the cows yield more, or less, milk. By this method, the goodness of the cheese is preserved and, without all dispute, it is the best cheese that England affords, if not, that the whole world affords.

Wookey, where the River Axe emerges from Wookey Hole, caves shown to have been occupied from prehistoric times and right through the Roman era, is a pleasant little village with a largely Perpendicular church and small Perpendicular chapel. The hand-made paper mills have been here since the seventeenth century, and remain discreet and undisturbing. In the distant past a curse is said to have been laid on the village by a spiteful witch who lived in Wookey Hole. A monk sent from Glastonbury sprinkled her with holy water, and she was at once petrified into the stalagmite known as the Witch of Wookey: every visitor has learned to recognize her nose and the cut of her bonnet.

Close to the Dorset border is the stone-built village of East Coker, which gave its name to the first of T. S. Eliot's *Four Quartets*. (The origin of another, Little Gidding, is to be found in Huntingdonshire.) The poet's ashes were laid in the church here in 1965.

Just over the border into Dorset is a little village which I propose to include for the sheer sake of its name—Ryme Intrinseca. This delightful formation merely means Ryme-within-the-boundaries, as opposed to a now forgotten Ryme Extrinseca, which was obviously beyond the pale. It seems fitting that its church should have the unusual dedication of St Hippolyte.

Dorset really does have some of the most resonant, provocative names. Sandford Orcas is another village with a finely haughty ring to it. The honey-coloured manor house is a beautiful Elizabethan building with a worthy gatehouse, and a long-standing reputation for being haunted. The present owners recount that on one occasion a visitor tried to pay his admission fee to an old man sitting near the stables when no such old man existed. It may have been the same figure as that of the tenant farmer who hanged himself from the gatehouse many years ago, wearing a white smock in which he is sometimes seen by guests and villagers on his perambulation through the grounds.

We are still in a world of thatched roofs. Straw and reed thatch went out of fashion for richer, more imposing houses many centuries ago, but has survived in the villages into our own time, encouraged to some extent by purchasers wanting to live in a truly rural atmosphere, and discouraged by insurance assessors who bump up premiums on the grounds of fire risk. Most thatchers—and there has been quite a revival of the craft in recent years—would deny there is any great risk.

Ditches on Sedgemoor yield the flexible shoots of osier which, when green, can be twisted without snapping and used in wickerwork—or, in the more distant past, to bind laths into the framework of a lath and plaster cottage. From the ditches also come reeds for thatching. Sedge is used for roof ridges of a reed thatch and sometimes, as in the Fens, for the entire roof. At Wicken in Cambridgeshire, generations of villagers cultivated narrow strips of sedge for thatch and animal bedding, and some of their open fields are preserved in the National Trust enclosure of Wicken Sedge Fen. The reed called Norfolk spear is in great demand from the Norfolk Broads and marshes. Even church roofs are to be seen thatched, as at Theberton in Suffolk; and I recall that in nearby Westleton two or three

11 *Fletching, Sussex*

years ago children were encouraged to contribute a personal share to re-thatching by 'investing' in a bundle of reeds at 10p a time.

Most parts of England use straw for roofs, but reeds are stronger and more durable, and can be packed more tightly against weather and the depredations of birds.

Reed is cultivated at Abbotsbury in Dorset, a mainly seventeenth-century village of warmly tinted stone behind the accumulating ridge of the Chesil Bank, and in the shelter of an ilex-covered hill where sub-tropical gardens were planted in the following century. The Abbotsbury swannery is estimated to hold the second largest herd in Europe, its numbers kept at between eight hundred and a thousand by a warden bearing the now rare designation of swan-herd.

There are other testimonies to older times and customs. Abbotsbury Castle is an Iron Age fort looking out from a commanding hilltop. St Catherine's Chapel, equally well placed for wide-ranging views, is massively buttressed to withstand the direct onslaught of the sea winds. Into one of its pillars young maidens would drop a pin as token that they wished a favour of St Catherine, such as the provision of a husband. Perhaps some of them still, secretively, do so. Built just as solidly is the fifteenth-century tithe barn, so huge that one can only assume the monks of the Benedictine abbey were sumptuously supplied with their needs by the farms of the locality.

Strong stone walls in Portisham are almost too much for the village, imprisoning rather than protecting it. It has a nice fifteenth-century, Perpendicular church with its original screen. A busy road towards Weymouth makes one end of the village street noisy, but from there it climbs up towards the heath and plantations of Wareham Forest. On the tip of Black Down stands what appears from miles around to be a huge factory chimney. This is the Hardy memorial—not a tribute to the novelist whose name will always be associated with this county, but to that Hardy who was Nelson's flag captain at Trafalgar and to whom the great admiral's dying words were addressed.

The other, Thomas Hardy, was born in the hamlet of Higher Bockhampton, three miles out of Dorchester in the parish of Stinsford which he immortalized as Mellstock in the idyllic *Under the Green-wood Tree*. The family had always been devoted to music, and played their part in the provision of instrumental accompaniment to church services. In addition, Thomas himself was in demand as a fiddle player at local dances and fêtes. *The Mellstock Quire*, sub-title of the above novel, is taken straight from his own experience and sings with the happiness of it. He was apprenticed to an ecclesiastical architect, and his training and practice in church restoration gave him another recurrent theme for his writing. It also took him on an early commission to St Juliot in Cornwall (known locally as 'St Jilt'), where the door of the rectory was opened to him by the rector's sister Emma . . . who became his wife in 1879. The village appears as Endelstow in *A Pair of Blue Eyes*.

Towards the end of his life Hardy felt despondently that his work had not been fully appreciated. But the pall-bearers at his funeral included some of the greatest writers of his day, and his ashes were interred in Westminster Abbey. His heart has a resting-place in the churchyard at Stinsford—though there is a tale that it is not, as it were, whole-hearted, having been gnawed by the surgeon's cat.

Stinsford's church of St Michael stands beside the sprawling manor house, now a school. It was much restored in the eighteenth century and again in the nineteenth, leaving its Norman font as almost the only significant relic. The thatched cottage in which Hardy was born and where he produced some of his earlier work is preserved at Higher Bockhampton on the edge of Thorncombe Wood, through which the Dorset Naturalists' Trust have laid out a very attractive nature trail.

This is on the western fringe of what the novelist christened Egdon Heath. One could spend many a happy hour penetrating various camouflages, some of them very flimsy, to identify the real places behind the fiction. Egdon Heath itself is in essence Winfrith Heath. From the village of Winfrith Newburgh, with a few Norman remains in its church, the little River Winfrith makes its way across the tangled bracken until it is sucked into an atomic power station whose presence would hardly have pleased the writer. The name Winfrith is Celtic for 'happy stream'. Not far away we find the house where

Tess of the d'Urbervilles spent her dismal wedding night with Angel Clare: it is Woodbridge Manor at Wool, now a hotel, on whose staircase can still be detected fading pictures of the actual Turbervilles. The Perpendicular church at Bere Regis, which merits a visit for the splendour of its carved nave roof, contains tombs of the Turbervilles.

There are associations with T. E. Lawrence. When he left the R.A.F. he bought a gamekeeper's cottage as his home, Cloud's Hill, near Bovington Camp. Killed in a motor-cycle accident in 1935, he is buried in the churchyard at Moreton. The bright little church itself has chancel windows engraved by Laurence Whistler.

So-called 'Purbeck marble', a crystalline limestone packed with minute shell fossils, was once much sought after for church and cathedral work, especially for internal use where its polish would not be spoilt by the weather. Transport to various destinations was simplified by the nearness of the sea to the peninsula of the Isle of Purbeck. A lot of basic carving was done before shipment, and most of this in the masons' houses of Corfe Castle.

The village spreads itself under the shadow of the castle, built by Edward 1 on the site of an earlier fortress where an earlier Edward was stabbed by his stepmother, Elfrida, in 978 so that her own son might become king. The village church is dedicated to him as St Edward, King and Martyr. Pale grey stone is relieved here and there throughout the tidy streets by an occasional splash of brickwork, as in the seventeenth-century town hall. It calls itself a town hall; but Corfe Castle is still a village. Its roofs frequently look impressive but alarming. Are the occupants of the houses entirely safe? Purbeck slate seems too weighty to use in roof tiling, and requires hefty supports. Even with these, the stones tend to sag into a pattern of gulleys and ripples, and are then pasted into new firmness by liberal applications of mortar.

Visitors to Dorset are invariably amused by the proliferation of Piddles and Puddles. They are all related to the River Pidele, which with the erosion of time has become the Piddle. Victorian prudes tried to re-fashion this to Puddle, so now there are derivatives of both. Piddlehinton, a flinty village with plenty of thatch, was once called Honey Puddle. Piddletrenthide, set along the vale and dominated by the lovely tower of its fifteenth-century church, has been explained as being a settlement thirty hides in area beside the River Piddle, and this would seem to be borne out by a thirty-hide assessment in Domesday Book. But it so happens that the Piddle is also known as the Trent, and I think there may be some justice in the theory of one Dorset native that it's simply a 'belt and braces' duplication. Puddletown shows signs of expansion in Victorian times, but retains many thatched, colour washed cottages. Cardinal Pole, the last Catholic Archbishop of Canterbury, was vicar for three years of the impressive church, whose tower has an external turret staircase. A heraldic window by Ninian Comper commemorates the Athelhampton family, whose restored fifteenth- and sixteenth-century Athelhampton Hall is open to the public on certain afternoons between April and September.

There are Affpuddle, Turners Puddle and Bryants Puddle. And of course there is Tolpuddle.

Robert Owen dreamed of creating one mighty representative body to unite all the workers in the land. In 1833 he was one of the founders of the Grand National Consolidated Trades Union, pledged to work towards a co-operative system. Although membership of such a union had now been legalized, six Tolpuddle farm labourers were arrested for attempting to join, on the grounds that they had administered an illegal oath when so doing. They were tried and, as an example to other dissidents, sentenced to seven years' transportation. Driven to the hulks at Portsmouth chained to the outside of a coach, they were duly shipped to New South Wales. Two years almost to the day after promulgation of the sentence, they were released in response to unrelenting public outcry.

A hundred years later the t.u.c. held its annual conference at Weymouth, and there was a ceremonial visit to the village to inaugurate six cottages for the aged, built and named in memory of the six pioneers. A shelter on the village green was also unveiled that day, 31 August 1934, and is still to be seen close to the 'Martyrs' Tree' where the men had formulated their plans. In the churchyard is the headstone of John Hammett, the only one to settle in Tolpuddle after his release: the others, after being set up on farms in Essex, were so harassed as 'ex-convicts' by local landowners and clergy that in disgust they finally emigrated to Canada.

In the folds of the chalk hills riding across central Dorset is Cerne Abbas. It once showed some sign of developing into a sizeable market and light industrial town, but gave up; and, unlike so many villages eager to achieve township status—or at best not struggling too gallantly to avoid it—has gracefully abandoned such pretensions as the follies they are. Some of its houses and part of the fabric of its inns are redolent of the Middle Ages, and the reinforcement of their structure owes much to the use of material from the Benedictine abbey ruins. There are several examples of oversailing upper storeys near the church, which has a sturdily buttressed tower sheltering a rare Madonna which somehow survived the Reformation. In the churchyard is a wishing well at which, for best results, you must turn your back on the Cerne Abbas giant, make a cup from a laurel leaf, and wish facing the church. The giant is a figure 180-ft high cut into the chalk, endowed with sexual organs so generous that monks of the abbey and rectors of the church preferred them to remain blurred by turf. It has been suggested that the outline is two thousand years old, associated with a fertility cult within the nearby earthwork of the Trendle—a word meaning, as in the Trundle at Goodwood, a hoop or circle. But other researchers associate the giant with a Romano-British conception of Hercules. 'Conception' strikes the right chord in this context: for centuries the maypole was set up above the giant's head, and barren women would lie beside him in the grass at night in the hope of becoming fertile.

Some miles to the east is the model village of Milton Abbas. The abbey from which it takes its name was presented by Henry VIII to the lawyer who picked a way through the complexities of the royal divorce from Catherine of Aragon. The lovely abbey church survives, restored by Sir Giles Gilbert Scott, together with a fifteenth-century sacrament house. Other remains, incorporating the abbot's hall, have become a school. The rectory formed the basis of a status-symbol manor which the first Earl of Dorchester decided to build for himself in the late eighteenth century. At the same time he set about transferring the existent village to its present woodland setting, laid out with formal grace on both sides of sloping greens. The cottages are in trim pairs with identical bonnets of thatch and neatly aligned chimney pots. A more recent bay window or two startle the eye with their interruption of the ordained regularity.

The highest village in Dorset, perched up on the rim of Cranborne Chase and looking out as far as the Isle of Wight on a clear day, is Ashmore. It has an embanked duckpond and a sparkling contrast of cottages and outbuildings—flint, brick, thatch and tile. The very name—'the mere of the ash tree'—has a reliable Saxon ring, but such a lofty settlement was rare for post-Celtic immigrants, and the place reverberates with echoes of earlier occupants. Romano-British villages have been identified all around, and this may have been another such, its nature and setting defined by lowland Saxons in the name they bestowed on it, but not occupied by them until after years of dereliction.

Another name, for the sheer sake of the name—Sixpenny Handley, giving its age away in this old union of two hundreds, Saxpena and Hamlega.

The green sandstone walls and roofs of the Blackmore Vale blend, across the Wiltshire border, in with the green-stippled oolites of the once busy quarries of Tisbury and Chilmark in the vale of the River Nadder. This is a valley of unpretentious beauties—though near the Fonthills there was once reared the most pretentious folly of Beckford's Fonthill Abbey, its over-ambitious tower continually crashing down in ruin. Teffont Magna and Teffont Evias make a charming pair, with the latter perhaps the prettier. Dinton, where the composer Henry Lawes was born, still retains the stone-built Lawes Cottage and many other preserved buildings which make the village almost a National Trust enclave: Dinton Park with Philipps House, now a Y.W.C.A. holiday home, farm cottages, the Tudor house of Little Clarendon, and eighteenth-century Hyde's House.

'All country people hate each other,' said William Hazlitt, and went on to declare that one could hope to find nothing but 'a perpetual round of mischief-making and backbiting for want of any better amusement'. Yet there were times when the countryside appealed to him more than the 'sweeteners of human life' he found in the town. Although his marriage to Sarah Stoddart was unhappy, she did at least bring to him a cottage at Winterslow, a spot which he found so agreeable that even after their divorce and in spite of some sour memories it must have held, he returned to stay for long periods at an inn then called the *Winterslow Hut*. His chief happiness, according to his son's introduction to the volume of essays named after the village, was the thorough quiet of the place, the sole interruption to which was the passage of the London mail coaches, announced from the hilltops in either direction by a flourish on the horn. It was here that Hazlitt, towards the end of his life, wrote:

> I have no need of book or companion—the days, the hours, the thoughts of my youth are at my side, and blend with the air that fans my cheek. Here I can saunter for hours, bending my eye forward, stopping and turning to look back, thinking to strike off into some less trodden path, yet hesitating to quit the one I am in, afraid to snap the brittle threads of memory.... I can easily, by stooping over the long-spent grass and clay-cold clod, recall the tufts of primroses, or purple hyacinths, that formerly grew on the same spot, and cover the bushes with leaves and singing-birds, as they were eighteen summers ago.

The inn is now the *Pheasant*, and there are more interruptions than those caused by the mail coaches: the road has become the A30.

When the seat of the diocese was shifted from Old Sarum early in the thirteenth century, the first man to be buried in the new Salisbury Cathedral was William Longespée, an illegitimate son of Henry II. His widow Ela, Countess of Salisbury, founded an Augustine nunnery at Lacock. At the Dissolution the buildings were granted to the Sharington family and converted into a Tudor mansion, which remained as the core of later embellishments. A daughter of the family married John Talbot, a descendant of the foundress, and the estate remained in the hands of this line until 1944, when Matilda Talbot presented the abbey, nearly three hundred acres of land, and most of the village to the National Trust.

It was here in 1835 that William Henry Fox Talbot invented a process without which the illustrations to this book would appear markedly different—if they existed at all. Following in the footsteps of Daguerre, he perfected a negative–positive process which he called calotype, making it possible to duplicate pictures in the form of prints. A great store of his early negatives and photographs were found in a cupboard at Lacock Abbey in 1937, and presented by Miss Talbot, his granddaughter, to the Science Museum in South Kensington.

The village is a beautiful relic of the prosperous wool industry, a harmony of stone, timber and brick. It has been called the loveliest village in England; but then so have several other clothiers' settlements in the neighbourhood. Many would award the palm to Castle Combe in its shaded vale, with golden stone in its cottages and bridges, and moss softening its tiled roofs. Sleepy with self-satisfaction around its fifteenth-century market cross, it had a somewhat traumatic awakening when a film company descended on it and temporarily converted it into an apparent sea-port for the film of *Doctor Dolittle*. This invasion bestowed one boon on the village, however : in place of the television aerials which were taken down during filming, the villagers have been provided with a wired system which no longer offends the eye.

The creamy stone of the Cotswolds runs through the whole string of wool towns and villages. It is a limestone whose softness is responsible for the gently undulating contours of the hills, and proves easy to work and to ornament when first quarried. Used both in walls and in roofing, its porosity means that roofs have to be pitched steeply in order to shed rain and snow before they can seep through. Churches in the region vie with one another in the extravagance of their carved stone 'beak-heads' of real and fantastic birds, their expressions usually sly or derisive. Even more startling on a place of Christian worship are the pagan figures on the church at North Cerney—creatures half man, half beast, leering even more knowingly than the beak-heads.

A little way along the Churn valley, Bagendon has a notable stone-roofed church with a saddle-back tower and some fine medieval remnants in its windows, including insignia of the weavers' guilds. The height of the altar above the nave floor level is due to the need

12   *Rolvenden, Kent*

to save it from frequent flooding, which has been known to keep the church waterlogged for days on end. Some Norman elements have been preserved, including the font, and in the tower is the grave-stone of a pre-Conquest man found beneath the church. But the village has far older relics than these. Excavations in the local gravel pit a couple of decades ago revealed a man-made stone surface, at first thought to be a section of some lost Roman road but then shown to be too extensive for that. As investigation proceeded, fragments of Belgic pottery and ornaments came to light. It has now been es-tablished pretty conclusively that this must have been the capital of the Dobunni tribe, hitherto ascribed to Cirencester; and even that far back, sheep were kept and cloth was woven.

There was a seventeenth-century wool factory at Bibury, formed from a terrace of cottages now known as Arlington Row. The adjoin-ing meadow is called Rack Isle because of the racks on which wool was hung out to dry. After a career of tweed manufacture, Arlington Mill turned to flour milling. It is now a rural museum. The village's incomparable main street runs parallel with the River Coln, rich in trout, and crosses the stream before the creeper-hung *Swan* hotel.

Bourton-on-the-Water—the water in this case being that of the Windrush—also has reason to be proud of its bridges, with diminu-tive parapets which would protect no one from falling in the stream on a dark night. The delightful riverside walk, a frieze of Cotswold stone, trees and lawns, is echoed in a scale model built behind the *New* inn, including a working mill and a replica of the inn itself. Outside the village, the Birdland Zoo Gardens display hundreds of foreign and exotic birds.

Perhaps the best centre from which to explore the by-ways and villages of the region is Snowshill, high up in the wolds. Its most striking feature is Snowshill Manor, an almost unspoilt Tudor house with a façade dating from the late seventeenth century, with a col-lection of weaving and spinning equipment, and some old clocks and musical instruments. In 1842 Charles Keyte of this village invented one of the earliest sewing machines, now lodged in the Science Museum in South Kensington.

One of the finest vistas of Herefordshire I ever saw was from the

15 *Kersey, Suffolk*

top of the Malverns when the sunset was blazing out over the Black Mountains and the marshes. Individual villages were lost in such a broad, exhilarating prospect; but a different, more intimate pleasure is offered when one comes down to the levels. Zummerzet is not the only county 'where the cider apples grow'. Nearly every farmstead and village here in Herefordshire has its orchard; and many have hop-yards, too, the only contenders of any size with those of Kent.

Also along this border are the most plentiful remaining examples of a style of timber construction which was once common in simple, cheap domestic buildings. Tree trunks or 'crucks' were driven into the ground and then bowed together at the top. Between two such arches a ridge pole was secured, and side timbers supported a combination wall and roof. Later this fundamental shape was adjusted to allow for more vertical walls, the inclusion of a second storey, and windows in place of small shuttered openings.

There is a fine surviving example of cruck framing in Weobley, next to the thirteenth-century *Red Lion* inn, where part of an old barn has been converted into a cottage without losing its distinctive old skeleton. Elsewhere in the village is a black-and-white richness of half-timbering, marking various developments of the box-frame type of house which superseded the cruck-frame. Timber uprights known as studs support a first floor, often with a protruding jetty, and further verticals support the roof, strengthened by horizontal beams to give a multitude of cross-hatched patterns. When timber grew scarce throughout the country because of the demands of the charcoal burners in the glass and iron industries, and of the ship-yards, the intervals between the upright studs grew wider.

There are other fine specimens at Eardisland beside the River Arrow, including fourteenth-century Staick House, which has additions made in later centuries in admirable keeping with the original, and now houses an interesting costume and curio exhibition.

Running below the border range of Wales, some of whose names have slipped inextricably among the English ones, is the Golden Valley of the River Dore. At its northern end is Dorstone, at the southern Abbey Dore. In the church at Dorstone is displayed a chalice taken from the tomb of its founder—Richard de Brito, one of the knights who murdered Thomas à Becket at Canterbury. Near the village is another of the supposed resting places of King Arthur—a prehistoric cromlech known as Arthur's Stone. The church of Abbey Dore, lapped in the blossom of its orchards in spring, has, as the village name implies, a monastic origin. In the twelfth century there was a Cistercian abbey here. Its church was restored in the early seventeenth century by Viscount Scudamore, the work including a fine oak screen for the chancel designed by John Abel, known as 'The King's Carpenter' for his services to Charles I during the siege of Hereford.

Cider production having for so long been one of Herefordshire's main industries, it is not surprising that so many glasses have been raised in so many villages on Twelfth Night in the old custom of wassail—drinking a toast to the health and plenitude of the fruit crop in the forthcoming year. 'Wassail': be fortunate.

CHAPTER FOUR

South and South-East

Two trackways run out of Hampshire to climb the slopes of chalk and sandstone ridges lying roughly parallel across southern England. The Pilgrims' Way begins at Winchester and for much of its route to Canterbury shares the path of the North Downs Way. The South Downs Way, reaching the sea at Beachy Head in Sussex, is not yet open all the way to Winchester, but it is hoped to achieve the necessary clearances fairly soon and even to take the footpath and bridleway on to Salisbury. Both ridgeway tracks skirt a succession of historic and prehistoric forts and settlements. And below the ridgeways are the villages of the river gaps, the woodlands and the Weald.

The north-eastern route from Winchester leads towards Alresford and Alton, but the curious traveller is almost immediately sidetracked by the name of Tichborne. There are monuments in the church to many generations of the family which bestowed this name on the village, and they are also remembered in the Tichborne Dole ceremonially distributed each Lady Day. This was instituted centuries ago by Lady Isabella Tichborne, who on her deathbed is said to have asked her husband for enough land to guarantee the financing of an annual gift of bread to the poor of the parish. He promised her as much as she could crawl round with a blazing torch in her hand. Lady Isabella managed to cover more than twenty acres before she died. But if this story is known to all the villagers, the story of the Tichborne claimant is known to the whole world. In 1872 Thomas Castro, a Wapping butcher commonly known as Bullocky Orton, claimed to be the missing heir to the Tichborne estates, and had swotted up the background with such care that for some time he convinced the real heir's mother of his genuineness. It is thought to have cost the family about £70,000 to contest the claim and finally reveal him as a fraud.

A little way up the valley of the Itchen—where, in fact, it rises—is Bramdean, which claims to be the scene of Alfred's last battle against the Danes. In 1825 William Cobbett had an experience there calculated to arouse his ever-responsive hackles:

> We stopped at the village to bait our horses; and, while we were in the public-house, an Exciseman came and rummaged it all over, taking an account of the various sorts of liquor in it, having the air of a complete master of the premises, while a very pretty and modest girl waited on him to produce the divers bottles, jars and kegs. I wonder whether Alfred had a thought of any thing like this, when he was clearing England from her oppressors?

And one wonders what Cobbett would have had to say about the magnitude and complexity of our present Excise duties, and above all of such devices as Value Added Tax.

To soothe his and our irascibility, best turn to two villages set not so far apart: Chawton and Selborne, each the home of quietly as-siduous workers who saw the whole of human and animal life in the microcosm of their apparently restricted surroundings. Jane Austen was born in 1775 in Steventon, another village of this county, where her father was rector for forty years. Jane, who is commemorated in his church by a memorial tablet, owed most of her schooling to her father. After his death in 1805 she and her mother and sister Cas-sandra lived for a while in Southampton and then settled in the cot-tage which her brother owned at Chawton. Her first three novels had been written at Steventon but only now came to be published; and during the eight years left to her she managed to write *Mansfield Park*, *Emma* and *Persuasion* in the sitting-room of the cottage, slip-ping the pages out of sight whenever the family or visitors appeared. Part of the cottage is now a museum. Mrs Austen and Cassandra are buried in the local church, but Jane herself lies in Winchester Cathedral, beneath an epitaph so sanctimonious that it would surely have brought a smile to her lips could she have been forewarned of it.

The village of Selborne is best viewed from the steep, beech-covered slopes of Selborne Hanger; and it was on these slopes that Gilbert White made several of his most significant observations. By patient concentration on the small, the local and the immediate he reached scientific conclusions of far more than local importance. He studied hibernation and migration; dissected cuckoos to find if some physical defect accounted for their unwillingness to hatch their own eggs; kept a journal and 'Garden Kalendar' of his findings; and wrote long letters to the naturalists Thomas Pennant and Daines Barrington, eventually published in book form as *The Natural History and Antiquities of Selborne*. He was a true villager at heart, reluctant to stray far from his own beloved paths and fields: ordained as a priest, he managed to obtain livings near Selborne, of which he became vicar in due course. He lived out his leisurely but inquiring life at the parsonage or his family home, The Wakes, and when he died in 1793 was buried in his own churchyard. The Wakes has become a joint library and museum for himself and a man who could hardly have been more different—the explorer Captain Oates, who accompanied Scott on his tragic Antarctic expedition and walked out into the alien wastes rather than be a burden on his companions.

Veering back to rejoin the Pilgrims' Way, we enter Surrey near Farnham and edge up towards the ridge of the Hog's Back through Sandy Cross. There is nothing along that race-track of dual carriageway to tempt the meditative. But below it, just escaping another monstrous main road, is Compton, comfortably set along its main street with two remarkable temptations to slow the traveller heading for Godalming. The church of St Nicholas has a unique double sanctuary with a Norman vault below and a separate chapel above, its balustrade being probably the only woodwork of its kind to have survived from Norman times. More flamboyant is the memorial chapel designed by the wife of G. F. Watts, the Victorian painter and sculptor—largely designed before he died, with a gilded and many-tinted interior in the most striking Art Nouveau style. This and the Watts picture gallery, housing a hundred and fifty paintings and other examples of his work, are open to the public all year round.

North of Chilworth the track passes St Martha's chapel, where pilgrims once stopped on their way towards Canterbury. In spite of its nineteenth-century restoration, traces of its Norman origin are still easy to find. And so, through Albury along the vale of the Tillingbourne to Shere. This boasts of being the most beautiful village in Surrey, and since being by-passed it may hope to retain those beauties; but whenever I hear anyone holding forth on this subject I am irresistibly driven to say, 'But wait until you see Chiddingfold.' A mistake: one ought to keep such subjective judgments to oneself. If, in Sussex, I prefer Northiam to popular Alfriston; in Suffolk, Chelsworth to Kersey; in Kent, Fordwich to much-photographed Chilham; then surely it is best to keep quiet so that I may enjoy these places while the majority do their visiting elsewhere? Which is not to denigrate Shere or any of the other places I have mentioned. Shere's church sits charmingly below the folds of the hills, with a fine shingled spire set on its Norman tower, and a lych-gate framing a sparkling corner of the village and a few yards of its main street. On the other side of the village green is the *White Horse* inn, and just outside the village on the far side of the by-pass is the Silent Pool, a tranquil mere in shady woodland—tranquil except on Bank Holidays, when there is a marked accumulation of soft drink cans, sweet papers and cigarette packets. Legend has it that King John rode one day to the pool because of rumours he had heard concerning the beauty of a local woodsman's daughter, and that when she tried to escape him she floundered into the deepest part of the water. Her brother dived in to rescue her, but she wrapped her arms round him in panic and drew both of them down to their death.

At Burford Bridge the Pilgrims' Way crosses the River Mole near the hotel, once known as the *Fox and Hounds*, where Keats completed *Endymion* and Lord Nelson spent his last night with Emma Hamilton before leaving for the battle of Trafalgar. We continue through Betchworth, where the scores of small lime kilns which existed in earlier centuries have been concentrated into great chalk pits lying right across the path, and on at last into Kent.

History crowds in on a key ford across the River Medway. On the downs above Aylesford is the great megalithic barrow of Kit's Coty House, reached by a path from the Pilgrims' Way. Below are scattered remnants of another burial chamber known as Little Kit's Coty House. At the ford itself, Hengist and Horsa, invited to settle in the country by King Vortigern, turned on their host at the place then called in the *Anglo-Saxon Chronicle* Agaelesprep or Aegelesford.

16 (above) *Cley-next-the-Sea, Norfolk*
17 (below) *Blakeney, Norfolk*

Horsa was slain. 'And after that Hengist succeeded to the kingdom and Aesc, his son.' Later, Edmund Ironside fought the Danes here. In the thirteenth century a Carmelite friary was founded by the riverside. Dissolved during the iconoclastic Tudor period, it was re-established in 1949, and now has a pottery, spacious grounds for visitors, and a generally cheerful air which seems evangelical rather than contemplative. Aylesford has kept its medieval bridge and medieval shape within a sprawl of light and not-so-light industrial growth, and narrow streets better seen late on a quiet evening than at busy midday. On the opposite bank is another kind of village at Preston Hall, a rehabilitation centre for invalid ex-servicemen.

The ancient route to Canterbury takes us by Charing, which has some ugly modern excrescences to deter the prospective visitor. It is worth persevering, however: within the village, beside the fourteenth-century church, are the gateway and other remains of an Archbishop's Palace where Cranmer entertained Henry VIII and some thousands of his retainers on their way to the Field of the Cloth of Gold.

Pilgrims would have continued through Chilham, where there is still a so-called Pilgrims' Cottage topped by a small bell-cote. The village square is rich in half-timbering and warm tiled roofs, with pub and church providing a classic English juxtaposition. Opening off one side of the square are the gates of Chilham Castle. In the grounds, laid out by Capability Brown, is a Norman keep; but the present building, which may have been the work of Inigo Jones, is essentially a Jacobean mansion rather than a fortress. A Battle of Britain museum of aero-engines, log-books and other material has been established here, complete with a restored Hurricane and a Messerschmitt. At certain times there are flying displays—not by aircraft but by eagles and falcons.

And so through Harbledown, where at Bigbury Camp the Britons were routed by Julius Caesar, and on into Canterbury, beyond which the North Downs Way continues in a loop towards the cliffs of Dover and back again through Dunn Street. Within its circumference are some pretty hamlets and some not so pretty, marred by the incongruous proximity of the Kent coalfields. Just outside Canterbury in the marshy valley of the Stour is a village which was once a busy town—port for the city, no less. It has a town hall and some stately merchants' buildings in its narrow streets. But Fordwich lost its civic status long ago, and now is visited only by canoes and other small craft. Its town hall has become a museum in which are displayed the old stocks, drums used by the press gang, and a ducking-stool. The crane used for the dipping of scolds, and for unloading building stone and other cargoes from barges, is still in position against an outer wall. The *George and Dragon* inn has long been noted for the quality of its food and atmosphere, perhaps equalled only by the nearby *Red Lion* at Wingham.

On St Swithin's Day in 1972 Lord Shawcross formally opened the uninterrupted eighty-mile stretch of South Downs Way from Beachy Head to Buriton. For the walker or rider doubtful of his or her ability to tackle this all at one go there are side paths leading down to some of the loveliest downland villages; and in the river gaps the trackway itself descends for some happy meanders on the levels.

Cut into the chalk, the Long Man of Wilmington looks down on a village which, like Cerne Abbas under its pagan giant, was once a monastic settlement. William the Conqueror presented large estates to his half-brother, Robert de Mortain, who in his turn offered the manor of Wilmington to Grestain Abbey in Normandy. The small priory did not even have to wait for Henry VIII to decree its dissolution: its French connection brought it under such suspicion during the Hundred Years War that it was abandoned, and later incorporated into a house which for a while served as the local vicarage. The present church has a Jacobean canopied pulpit, and in the churchyard stands a yew which may be older than the building itself. As for the Long Man, he is said to have been a giant killed in a tussle with another giant, a Saxon war-god, and an academic hoax. His lack of sexual organs such as his Cerne Abbas cousin boasts has been ascribed to the more puritanical outlook of the monks or their successors in this region, who castrated him by turfing over the offending parts.

In the vale of the Cuckmere lies Alfriston—Aelfric's hamlet. There must have been a substantial early Saxon settlement here, for when foundations were being dug for a house there was revealed a large cemetery. Among the disjointed skeletons was one of a wealthy woman buried with her personal treasures, now preserved in the Sussex Archaeological Society's museum in Lewes. The fourteenth-century church of St Andrew is built in the shape of a Greek cross and incorporates characteristically the flints which, say resentful ploughmen, 'grow' out of the downland fields no matter how assiduously you try to clear them. Stone slates known as Horsham slabs once covered the roof, but these proved too heavy and have been replaced with tiles. The tower has a shingled cap, loftier and more graceful than most in the region. In the parish registers there are records of marriages as far back as 1504, which may well make this the oldest remaining marriage register in the country.

Smugglers once made good use of the Cuckmere, and their presence is well attested in *Market Cross House* and the famous *Star* inn, with its red wooden lion figurehead—thought to have come from a seventeenth-century wreck not far along the coast.

One of the village's smallest houses is also one of its most interesting. The Old Clergy House is a rare survival of a priest's home of pre-Reformation days. Used for generations as a labourer's cottage, it was sinking into disrepair when bought by the National Trust, the first building to be so purchased after the Trust's foundation in 1895.

Ditchling Beacon is one of the many unmistakable landmarks along the South Downs Way. The village below has one of the houses which Henry VIII gave to Anne of Cleves as payment for her consent to a divorce, with an accompanying chapel and attractive walled garden. Ditchling has attracted many distinguished residents, including Frank Brangwyn and Esther Meynell; and on its village green has a statue of a mother and child commemorating the work of James Young, the gynaecologist.

Chanctonbury Ring, with its circlet of beeches planted by Charles Goring while still at school and which he lived to see mature, is the most compelling reference point of all. The composer John Ireland wished to live always in sight of it, and is buried in Shipley churchyard within easy range. Much of his music was inspired by natural phenomena and places, and his *Amberley Wild Brooks* is a tribute to

the twisting and flooding waterways around one of the most capti-
vating villages on our route. Brick, tile, flint and thatch nestle in the
winding vale of the Arun. Amberley's castle was once an episcopal
palace, fortified in the fourteenth century but never having to face
siege or bombardment: much more appropriate to this setting is the
snug little manor house tucked away within the shelter of its ruined
walls and gatehouse.

Resting places for the walker are strung out below the South
Downs near Goodwood—once Godwin's Wood, owned by King
Harold's father. It was one of these hospitable little villages, Charlton, which was largely responsible for the creation of Goodwood. In
the eighteenth century the Charlton Hunt was the most celebrated
in the country, and it was during his forays with it that the first Duke
of Richmond decided to build himself a hunting lodge on the hilltop,
later to become a mansion with its own accompanying racecourse.
East Dean village lies below a slope of Celtic lynchets, and was itself
originally a Saxon clearing cut from the forest by swineherds from
the settlement of Singleton. The seventeenth-century flint houses,
with quoins of red brick relieving their sombreness, are darkened
again by slate roofs which replaced thatch after a severe fire in 1852.
West Dean, another Saxon swine pasture, is also all flint, with a
large grey mansion in spacious parkland where Edward VII used to
stay when attending race meetings, now a residential college for the
teaching of old and new English crafts.

In local churches and country houses are frequent specimens of
ornamentation in Sussex marble, a large part of it coming from the
quarries near Petworth. Locally it used to be known as winkle-stone,
since the Petworth variety was mainly formed from periwinkle
shells. Another type is sometimes known as cockleshell marble.

The South Downs Way runs out of Sussex near the Hartings, beneath the splendid park and mansion of Uppark, and reaches its
present terminal at Buriton. This Hampshire village sprays out a
number of footpaths into Queen Elizabeth's Forest and up the nine
hundred feet of Butser Hill. The Georgian manor house was the
scene of Edward Gibbon's boyhood years and much of his education,
since for some time it was found impossible to send him away to

school. In 1752 he went up to Oxford, but was soon expelled for outrageous behaviour and sent by his indignant father to a Calvinist minister's house in Switzerland. In Lausanne in 1764 he met the man who was to become his closest friend and patron—the Earl of Sheffield. Gibbon spent long periods at Sheffield Park, an estate now laid out as a comprehensive collection of trees and flowering shrubs and administered by the National Trust: here he wrote much of *Decline and Fall of the Roman Empire*, and when he died in 1794 was buried a few miles away in the Sheffield mausoleum in Fletching church.

Between the two major downland ridges lie the undulating lowlands of which the greater part, right across Sussex and Kent, is known as the Weald, from the impenetrable wood or wild of pre-Saxon times. Today it is an expanse of farmland—arable land, pasture, hop-gardens and orchards, market gardening—with lanes winding into convolutions inexplicable by modern standards, and little hamlets and farmsteads with names surprisingly often incorporating references to kilns, cinders, forges and hammers. It all looks as deeply rural as can be; but was for centuries the industrial heart of England.

On its Surrey fringe is Chiddingfold, with a vast green and spacious houses set back behind well-tended gardens. Red-tiled roofs, tile-hung frontages, a duckpond, a comfortably squat little church ... and a wonderfully timbered inn facing the village pump. The *Crown* was originally a thirteenth-century rest house for pilgrims travelling from Winchester to Canterbury; but by the end of the following century it had been let to a brewer, and has served as an inn ever since. The exterior matched many neighbouring buildings with its tile-hanging until 1951, when restoration disclosed the older half-timbering now happily exposed to view. But the real key to Chiddingfold's *raison d'être* is to be found in a lancet window in St Mary's church.

This window contains fragments of medieval glass taken from the rubbish tips of the abandoned glassworks on which this region once thrived. For here in the thirteenth century Lawrence Vitrarius— Lawrence the Glass-maker—bought land and went so wholeheartedly to work that before long Chiddingfold glass was famous throughout England and winning fame abroad. The windows of St Stephen's chapel at Westminster and St George's chapel at Windsor were commissioned from here. Other craftsmen learned from the imported foreign experts, of whom there were so many that entire church services at Wisborough Green were often conducted in French. The villages of Loxwood and Kirdford took their share of the prosperity. At one period it looked as if Venetian and German competitors might overtake the manufacturers of the Surrey–Sussex border, but there was an injection of fresh talent when Huguenot refugees arrived in the middle of the sixteenth century. A plaque in Alfold churchyard commemorates Jean Carré, who introduced significant changes into the manufacture of Venetian-style glass.

Unfortunately the glass-makers' furnaces used a lot of fuel, leading to a conflict with the iron-founders. The apparently indestructible forest of the Weald was fast disappearing: timber was needed for the ships of the Tudor navies, and for furnaces throughout the whole area. In 1615 the iron-masters succeeded in having an Act passed to prohibit the use of wood fuel in glass manufacture, thereby strangling the industry. Villagers resorted either to farming or, more profitably, to the industry which had defeated their own.

There are several indications of Romano-British attempts to exploit the iron ore of the Weald, but they did not penetrate far into the forest, and it was not until the Middle Ages that intensive extraction began. The tranquil 'hammer ponds' of hamlets such as Friday Street, Slaugham and Cowden once streamed over waterwheels to work bellows and drive hammers, or sizzled and seethed around cooling iron.

It was supposedly near Buxted in 1543 that

> Master Huggett and his man John
> They did make the first cannon.

The village of Buxted still has a Hogge House; but the 'man John' is more likely to have been a French expert, Peter Baude, who worked closely with Hogge-Huggett. They were founders of a long Wealden tradition of cannon and shot manufacture for the Tudor navies and for later battles with the Dutch. A 'jack of the clock' at Abinger Hammer symbolizes the days when furnace and forge were hard at work all along the Tillingbourne valley, before giving way to unwarlike expanses of watercress beds. The floor of the nave in Wadhurst church is dark with cast-iron grave slabs, and there is a modern steel and glass screen in memory of the local industry. On the north-west, still verdant, corner of Ashdown Forest, West Hoathly has iron memorials on floor and walls to a family of iron-masters who lived a few miles from the village in Gravetye Manor.

Set cosily away behind a number of small hills and the rocky out-crops which have given rise to such freaks as 'Big-on-Little', West Hoathly gives the impression of being a place which, if cut off for weeks by snow or some natural catastrophe, might not even notice that it was no longer in touch with the outside world. It is neat, compact and securely founded, so well content with existence that it showed no great concern over the fact that its church had no traceable dedication. Not until 1925 was it discovered that a thirteenth-century deed made the grant of the land specifically to the church of St Margaret. Church and manor once belonged to Lewes Priory, and after the Dissolution were given to Thomas Crom-well. When he fell, as so many did, from Henry VIII's favour, it was added to the list of the king's gifts to Anne of Cleves. One wonders if Henry also presented Anne with suitably fast and comfortable coaches so that she might visit all her properties at reasonable in-tervals! The church has a fine shingled spire, once of oak but now of Canadian cedar. The whole roof was once of heavy Horsham slabs, but only the lower courses were retained during nineteenth-century restoration. Similar slabs can still be seen on the old Priest's House behind its little garden. The building is now administered by the Sussex Archaeological Society as a domestic and local craft museum.

Ashdown Forest itself was for so long a royal forest under the chase laws that few settlements of any size developed in it. Many of its hamlets owed their rejuvenation to the iron industry. Hartfield and Newbridge had water-powered furnaces and hammers, and Shef-field Park Ironworks built up a labour force of twenty-six men. But spoil of the woodlands was so great, and replanting so inadequate, that great tracts became heath and scrub. Heavy industry, along with the wool trade and others, moved away to the coal-rich North and Midlands.

Maresfield, standing on the southern rim of the forest at a crossroads which the London to Eastbourne traffic makes hideous during the summer months, was one of the royal manors whose free tenants were allowed grazing concessions and the right to glean fallen timber. It was also from here that timber was taken in large quantities for repairs at Pevensey Castle and its chapel. Maresfield had a free chapel to serve the royal hunting lodge near by, and a Maresfield family at one stage were appointed hereditary holders of the post of Master of the Game. It had an important forge, and in this church, too, are some iron grave slabs.

The forge, or rather a number of errors concerning it, has led to some fascinating recent speculation. Not far from Maresfield is Pilt Down, where Charles Dawson 'discovered' the supposed missing evolutionary link named after him. After this was proved a forgery, there were still doubts about the identity of the forger : was Dawson himself a guilty man or a dupe? Examination of another of his 'discoveries' overwhelmingly suggests the former. In 1912, the same year in which he first produced skull fragments from the gravel diggings on Pilt Down, he published an article accompanied by what he claimed to be a copy of a 1724 map of Maresfield Forge and its surroundings. This has now been compared with authentic maps of that year and later, and shown to be a hoax—and a clumsy one at that. The style of script belongs to a later century; the sketch includes a road which was not laid until 1830, a mill-pond not dug until at least 1880, and marks belonging to later Ordnance Survey conventions; and the furnace itself is demonstrably in the wrong place.

Iron was extracted and worked all the way across the Weald to Lamberhurst, from which came the railings for St Paul's Cathedral; Brenchley; and Horsmonden. Between these latter two lies Furnace Pond, a spacious hammer pond whose banks are now the resort of fishermen rather than foundrymen. Brenchley has a wealth of Tudor timbering which escaped the furnaces, and a post office which was once part of 'Roberts Mansion' or the Old Palace of the Duke of St

Albans. Horsmonden—which, like many neighbours with a similar suffix, takes the local accent on the last syllable as Horsmon*den*—has a gun outside the village inn, itself called the *Gun*, in memory of the Wealden Black Country era. It has a wide green, but something is wrong with its skyline. Church and churchyard, which should surely be planted to one side of this green, are quite a way from the village in the direction of Goudhurst. We have met Jane Austen in Hampshire: here in Kent lived her ancestors, prosperous clothiers.

Villages and homesteads of this eastern plain of the Weald retain more echoes of the wool trade than of iron, though several of them have depended at various times on both. Cloth halls, small-scale factories for the weavers, developed from the individual homesteads in which families used the central hall for most of their communal life, including work at their looms. Biddenden has a fine seven-gabled hall—and also, of course, a village sign commemorating the Siamese twins born here about 1100 and surviving, unusually for those days, to the age of thirty-four. In their will they left land to provide a dole for the poor of the parish, and their image is still baked into cakes every Easter Monday.

The administration of wills was different in this part of Kent from that in the rest of the country. Before the Norman Conquest land had been held under a law known as gavelkind, by which an inheritance was divided between all surviving sons of the deceased instead of going completely to the eldest. After the Conquest, estates presented to William's followers were usually freed from this, but in many farming areas it was allowed to continue. As a result, land did not fall into fewer and fewer hands but was shared out into manageable sections under the control of hard-working, independent yeomen farmers. They built themselves tall timbered dwellings which are usually described by the generalization, 'yeomen's houses'. The main feature was a central hall rising through the centre of the house—whence the other name, hall-houses—which in later times was often floored in to bring it into line with the two-storey construction of the rest of the building. These noble constructions appear singly or backed by outhouses in a setting of orchards and hop-gardens in 'The Garden of England', or as proud neighbours in the long village streets of the Weald. Smarden is perhaps the loveliest. But the cloth halls of Headcorn take some beating, and I have a soft spot for the place anyway: when I was a boy I used to pass it in the train on my way to holidays in Rye, and in later life commuted for a few years along this line. In effect it has only one side to its long main thoroughfare, the other being occupied by the wide approach to the railway station, a car park, and other open space. The passer-by sees it, from the train, as a colourful, irregular pattern of colours and roof-lines, rather as the motorist on the A12 sees the Suffolk village of Stratford St Mary strung out below him. But in Headcorn the houses do close in again, quite beautifully, at the approach to the church where the road swings right. And there is a thousand-year-old oak, a last mighty survivor of the Wealden forest.

The railway and many roads run towards Ashford and, beyond that, out on to Romney Marsh. There could hardly be a greater contrast than that between the settlements of the inland levels and those of the Romney, Denge, Walland, East Guldeford and Pett Levels. In the Weald the villages are lazy under the opiate of fruit blossom. On the wide littoral known to its inhabitants and lovers simply as 'The Marsh' the trees are thickly functional: windbreaks for hamlets whose impressive church towers are often quite concealed within the protective foliage. Most of the villages are at crossroads, and apparently minor crossroads at that. To make sense of the network of unhedged lanes, sharp turns, dykes and ditches and windswept huddles of unassertive cottages, one needs time, patience—and a bicycle. Walking between these scattered hamlets takes too long and, if attempted across the fields, involves too many frustrating detours: 'The Marsh is just-about riddled with diks and sluices, an' tide-gates an' water-lets,' as we learn from the tale of the Dymchurch Flit in Kipling's *Puck of Pook's Hill*. 'You'd think nothing easier than to walk end-on across her? Ah, but the diks and the water-lets they twists the roads about as ravelly as witch-yarn on the spindles. So ye get all turned round in broad daylight.' Yet from a car one gets too swift and misleading an impression of apparently

featureless plains: the villages slip by leaving no trace of their distinctive feel, sound and smell.

R. H. Barham, author of *The Ingoldsby Legends*, was for some years
curate of Warehorne and rector of Snargate. He chose to live in
the former rather than right out in the ague-ridden heart of the
dank levels, and delivered himself of the opinion that 'The world
is divided into five parts—Europe, Asia, Africa, America and Romney
Marsh'. The marshmen undoubtedly considered themselves a race
apart, claiming—and winning—many privileges from successive
monarchs, running their own courts with their own bailiffs and
jurats, and collaborating both with the patriotic navies of the Cinque
Ports when it suited them and with the smugglers whose word was
law across this territory. In Barham's own day, wrote his son,

> Many a time was the genial Rector, on returning home at night,
> challenged by a half-seen horseman who looked in the heavy
> gloom like some misty condensation, a little more substantial than
> ordinary fog, but on making known his name and office he was
> invariably allowed to pass on with a 'Goodnight, it's only parson,'
> while a long and shadowy line of mounted smugglers, each with
> a horse laden with tubs, filed silently by.

A doctor living at Brookland in 'Tom Ingoldsby's' day was often
summoned to treat the wounds of Customs officers and smugglers
who had come to grief in some bloody clash. The introduction of
armed 'blockade men' led to increasing violence, and in February
1821 to a pitched battle outside Brookland. A smuggling gang based
on Aldington had completed a successful landing, but were inter-
cepted by Preventive men and forced to fight it out. The blockade
officer and two of his men were killed, as against four smugglers
killed and sixteen wounded, before guides skilled in the convolutions
of the marsh led the free-traders to safety, apart from some unfortu-
nates who were seized and sent for trial at the Old Bailey.

Brookland village provides one of the few immediately recognizable landmarks other than the unsightly line of pylons stalking
towards the foothills from Dungeness nuclear power station. In its

churchyard the tall shingled pyramid of the bell tower stands apart from the largely Early English church. The most popular explanation for this is that the tower—or, rather, three-tiered spire—fell off the main building in amazement when a virgin and a spotless bachelor arrived to be wed. More prosaic versions have it that the belfry was twice set on the church and twice blown off, or that its additional weight would have proved too much for the spongy mound raised from the marshland. The original square framework was extended into an octagon in the middle of the fifteenth century, supposedly with the use of timbers from local shipwrecks. Today it holds a peal of five bells, one dating from the time of the tower's expansion, the others re-cast or newly made in 1685.

Inside the church is a Norman lead font which, in view of the building's dedication to St Augustine, may have been donated by a devout Norman pilgrim on his way to St Augustine's at Canterbury; or may equally well have been a piece of loot from one of the innumerable cross-Channel raids launched by men of the Cinque Ports against the French coast. Another association with Canterbury is the fragmentary medieval wall painting, discovered in 1964, of Becket's martyrdom.

Eighteenth-century tithe weights and measures are kept in a glass case, and there is also a hudd from about the same period—a sort of portable sentry-box within which the parson could conduct a graveside service without having his wig blown away into a sheep-pen or drenched by rain.

Brenzett's church of St Eanswythe—a daughter of King Eadbalde credited with being able to cast out devils and make water run uphill—is too large for its hamlet. The same could be said of Fairfield, Snave, Newchurch and others, now amalgamated into the Romney Marsh Group of Parishes and served in rotation by a panel of parsons. Several have old horse-box pews and are noted for their painted wooden text-boards, of which massive Ivychurch has an unfairly disparaging example: 'How dreadful is this place.' In the little churchyard of St Mary-in-the-Marsh, a short way inland from the holiday-camp clamour of St Mary's Bay and Dymchurch, a wooden barge-board carved by Captain Tucker marks the grave of his wife—previously Mrs Hubert Bland, otherwise E. Nesbit, author of *The Treasure Seekers* and *The Railway Children.*

Appledore sits just north of the Royal Military Canal where the levels and the ground begin to slope gently up to the foothills. The Military Road running parallel to the waterway from Rye joins a road across the bridge from the Marsh, and together they squeeze up a narrow street which abruptly opens out before the church and two attractive inns.

The village's present inland setting is deceptive. Before a mighty storm wrenched the course of the River Rother towards its present exit near Rye, Appledore probably stood on the tip of a low spit of land almost enclosing shallow saltings, with the neighbouring Isle of Oxney at times quite literally an island. Theories have been advanced about a possible Roman fort here, but this seems unlikely: Lympne, on higher ground and with a better anchorage, provided a much better situation for surveillance of the Saxon Shore. There were, however, both Saxon and Danish earthworks, and the *Anglo-Saxon Chronicle* names Apuldre as one of the main landing places for 'the great host' which in A.D. 893 came with Haesten in eighty ships. In spite of Alfred's repeated attempts to dislodge them, the Danes took a heavy toll of animals, foodstuff and human life in their occupation of the region, and after a while Appledore and other villages were abandoned, not to be resettled until the invaders turned their attention elsewhere.

Conflict with France in the fourteenth century brought fresh destruction. During one of their repeated coastal raids the French burned the village and the church: some of the original charred timbers were disclosed when work was being carried out in 1925. In rebuilding after the disaster, the church was left without a north aisle arcade, the whole northern span of the roof being taken up to a high ridge which throws the whole appearance off balance.

Later troubles with the French resulted in the digging of the Royal Military Canal, denounced by Cobbett and others as one of Pitt's most ludicrous follies. Whatever its failings, it did Appledore a power of good. During construction from Shorncliffe to the far rim of Pett Level a great deal of unhealthy marshland was drained.

Appledore found itself not only in a position of fair importance along the military and trading route of the canal, but also able to farm its fields with more hope of reward and less fear of disease than hitherto. In 1935 a sylvan stretch of bank between Appledore and Warehorne was presented to the National Trust.

Behind the village the road leads up towards Woodchurch, its little hill crowned by neighbourly church and pub. Gardens are bright with aubrietia and wallflowers, and at times the pub frontage is almost obscured by looping and weaving wisteria.

Along the undulating ridge to the east is Aldington, once the head-quarters of a notorious smuggling gang operating across the Marsh so enticingly spread below. Incorporated in the church pulpit is the carving of a pelican which was rescued about a hundred years ago from a local farmhouse, where it had been whitewashed and played some mysterious rôle in a children's game. Reminiscent of church musicians such as Hardy wrote about in the faraway West Country, a glass case near the font preserves some lovingly handwritten music and a number of musical instruments from the days when services were bolstered by a band in the west gallery.

Early in the sixteenth century a girl named Elizabeth Barton worked in an Aldington inn. After a serious illness she suffered recurrent bouts of religious hysteria, seeing visions and making prophecies. Some monks of Canterbury, including one Edward Bocking, were quick to publicize her as the Holy Maid of Kent, saintly symbol against the rising tide of Protestantism, especially when Henry VIII's determination to wed Anne Boleyn threatened the whole authority of the Roman Catholic Church in England. Elizabeth's personality was evidently very compelling: even Wolsey was afraid of her, and Henry himself summoned her to his presence for a personal talk. She predicted that within a few months of his marriage to Anne Boleyn he would be dead, backing this up with the assertion that she had received a communication to that effect from Mary Magdalen, written in gold lettering. The non-fulfilment of the prophecy lost her a great deal of popular support, and Henry struck before there could be any resurgence of confidence in her: she was arrested, declared to be a fraud and—by Sir Thomas More—

a 'lewd nun', and finally executed at Tyburn along with Bocking and other accomplices.

Another local spot which has associations with the Holy Maid is the remaining shred of Bellerica Chapel near Court-at-Street, on the road towards Lympne.

Lympne has a castle-cum-manor, restored and extended from eleventh- and fifteenth-century fabric, set precipitously on a steeply shelving cliff above Romney Marsh. From below, it is a squared-up cardboard cut-out against the skyline; behind, it shelters a cluster of cottages, some embedded in the castle wall and approached by a side lane with all the atmosphere of a private manorial drive. On the slopes which now face out across the levels but once looked out to sea above the installations of a busy military harbour are the crumpled walls and scattered stones of *Portus Lemanis*, looking as if some irritable giant had dislodged and kicked them down from the scarp above. They are all that remains of one of the forts which the Romans built to defend the coast against Saxon sea-raiders, on the sites of strongpoints established during the brief reign of the Belgic rebel against Rome, Carausius. The name derives from the River Limen, later to be renamed the Rother.

Near the church lychgate, close beside the entrance to the castle, is a little block of mounting steps for the benefit of those who had come to church on horseback. And where the road swings round and steeply down towards the Marsh is a monument to the proud past— the Shepway Cross, erected in 1923 by the then Lord Warden of the Cinque Ports to mark the spot where the barons of the Cinque Ports met in the Court of Shepway to discuss administration of their towns and defence of their privileges.

If we now turn our backs on the south coast and travel towards the northern shores of Kent, the scenery undergoes a drastic change. Along the Thames and well into the Medway are the paper manu-factories, quarries and engineering works which have engulfed old villages and old farmland. And, above all, there are the bleached lunar landscapes created by Aspdin's discovery in the 1830s of the way to make Portland cement, so called because of its supposed resemblance to Portland stone.

Lost in the dust of the chalk pits there is a village called Stone. Or once it was a village. Now it is probably best described as an industrial complex. But before racing towards and into the Dartford Tunnel, one should make a detour and seek out the church of St Mary—the 'Lantern of Kent'. Grimacing gargoyles sneer at the chimneys and whiten with a chalk film rather than with age. Inside, the church gives an eerie, fantastic impression of being larger than it was outside. Everything is high, airy and splendid. There are carvings in the stone of branches and stiff-leaf foliage, and interlaced arcadings. The date of the church's construction—about 1250 to 1260—and the whole style of it have led experts to believe it the handiwork of the men who rebuilt Westminster Abbey for Henry III.

It is the last oasis before we tackle either the suburban sprawl of London, which has engulfed so many villages and is still not satisfied, or the tunnel beneath the Thames to Essex.

19 *West Wycombe, Buckinghamshire*

CHAPTER FIVE

East Anglia and Neighbours

The landscape on the Essex bank of the Thames is a carbon copy of that on the Kent side, if there can be such a thing as a chalk-white carbon. To escape it one has to go a fair way to the east, to the sailing hamlets of the creeks and estuaries; and this involves negotiating —or somehow avoiding—the persistently reappearing main roads to Southend and Clacton.

Squeezed by industrial wastelands in the south, and threatened by London encroaching from the west, the true Essex survives at its best north of the A12. Writtle has become virtually a suburb of Chelmsford, and a large proportion of its population deserts it in the daytime to commute to London; but it remains at heart a village, with green and duckpond, and a largely Georgian surround of attractive houses. The eight Rodings—High, White, Leaden and more besides—are sprinkled about the River Roding, taking its name from the settlement of the Hrothingas. It is easy to pass through these farming hamlets without even noticing they are there; and the inhabitants, far from taking offence, are probably grateful. Another attractive cluster is that of the Bardfields, though these are of more substance : Great Bardfield was once a prosperous market town, and has prosperous-looking Georgian houses to prove it, together with an agreeable Cottage Museum containing exhibitions of local crafts and documents.

Black Notley and White Notley have little to offer in themselves, but Black Notley deserves to be saluted as the birthplace of John Ray or Wray in 1628. Son of the village blacksmith, Ray promoted a new approach to botanical studies at Trinity College, Cambridge, and in 1660 published a catalogue of local plants. Two years later he resigned his fellowship, published treatises on botany and zoology, and founded the system of naming species by two Latin words which was developed by Linnaeus and others into the present accepted worldwide usage.

20 (above) *Whitchurch, Oxfordshire*
21 (below) *Broadway, Worcestershire*

But the showpiece village of the county is, unavoidably, Finching-field. I am reminded of a friend whose job it has been for many years to lure foreign tourists to Denmark but who refuses ever to go and see the Copenhagen mermaid for himself: it has become so popular, appeared on so many posters and brochures and souvenir ashtrays, that he will not demean himself by visiting the real thing. Or so he says. I suspect that he has sneaked off to see the little lady on her rock more than once—and, to his dismay, found her more adorable each time. So it is with Finchingfield: no use saying it's too pretty to be true, because there it is, just as pretty as a picture, before your very eyes. From the bridge and green of this true green village the main street curves uphill between a charming variegated, uneven, sloping and slanting assortment of houses to the squat tower of the church, topped with a cheeky cupola. Beside the church is the early sixteenth-century Guildhall, a timber-framed cottage with a gateway from street to churchyard.

Standing at a strategic spot by the green, the visitor can glimpse both the church and, on a sharply rising mill-hill, the restored post-mill. The buck of this is set on a circular brick base with a conical wooden roof. There is no fantail to turn it: the body had to be faced into the wind by hand or by a horse attached to the pole jutting out behind. Near by is the so-called Round House, actually hex-agonal, which was devised by an eighteenth-century squire as a model cottage.

As we move across the county towards the Suffolk border we approach the nucleus of another of the major weaving communities. It is also a region in which nature seems to imitate art: it is impos-sible to look at any aspect of it without adjusting the present actuality to the more powerful reality of John Constable's paintings.

The world is wide: no two days are alike, nor even two hours; neither were there ever two leaves of a tree alike since the crea-tion of the world.

So said, and saw, the painter son of a Dedham Vale miller. Con-stable spent his life trying to capture on canvas or paper a joy which he knew must be for ever flying: the immediacy of a scene which would have changed before he could make a single stroke of his brush. His success was in itself a contradiction of what he asserted. For most of us, Dedham church tower is frozen and immaculate in eternity, with the twist of the Stour just so, the bend of this bank and that clump of trees just so.

When we get closer to the real Dedham we find that the tower is not an integral part of the church but a separate construction set against the west end, with an arch through to the churchyard, its ceiling decorated in relief with a luxuriant pattern of heraldic symbols.

There is more heraldry in the roof of the nave. Angels which once emerged from the bosses were struck down by the Crom-wellian iconoclasts, to be replaced in 1960 by shields testifying to various ecclesiastical and secular associations: the Tudor rose as symbol of the Duchy of Lancaster; tributes to the dioceses of Rochester, St Albans and Chelmsford; a Maria monogram echoing the church's dedication to the Blessed Virgin Mary; the link with Dedham, Massachusetts; and, among others, the most appropriate insignia of the Guilds of Weavers and Millers whose prosperity made possible the creation of such edifices. Some modern pews include one with medallions commemorating the first Moon landing in July 1969.

The village itself is concentrated along High Street, with some fine Georgian brick houses—two of them run together were once a grammar school—and the early sixteenth-century *Sun* inn, with an entrance for coaches into a spacious and attractive yard. Sherman's Hall is an example of a fairly plain brick house to which a new façade was added in the 1730s. The heavy embellishments include shallow columns like an exaggerated proscenium arch, emphatic window surrounds, a deep niche which ought surely to hold a statue of some goddess or philanthropist, and a parapet raised in the centre to accommodate a sundial.

Mill Lane strikes off towards the Stour, with the church of Strat-ford St Mary lifted on its knoll as if to peer anxiously across the dual carriageway which now slices between itself and its village. John Constable's father owned a watermill at Dedham and one at

Flatford; but it was not here that the family originally crossed the river from one county to another. The painter's great-grandfather left Essex to make his home in Bures early in the eighteenth century. John himself was born at East Bergholt, in whose churchyard his parents are buried. It was at Bergholt rectory that John was formally introduced to young Maria Bicknell, granddaughter of the well-to-do rector, whom in due course he married despite the opposition of her parents and grandfather. He travelled, wrestled with new themes and new obsessions, slowly established a reputation in the face of scorn and incomprehension; but came back again and again to the sources of his earliest inspiration—the towpaths of the Stour, East Bergholt Common, Dedham Vale seen from every angle. Although religious paintings were in popular demand, he made only two unimpressive attempts at such themes. One of them is to be found in the parish church of St James at Nayland.

Nayland village exhibits many characteristic Suffolk features. It has some sagging half-timbered houses with over-sailing upper storeys, colour washes including the ubiquitous 'Suffolk pink', and some touches of pargeting—ornamentation raised from or indented into plasterwork with a comb or trowel, employed with varying degrees of sophistication throughout the county. The village street widens near the church into what we might assume to have been a marketplace in bygone days. In fact there were two parallel streets here, now amalgamated to form a fine, broad vista. The Guildhall in High Street was the home of the cloth guilds, and it was a clothier named William Abel who built the church porch and a bridge across the Stour on which he left his signature in the form of a letter A followed by the sketch of a bell.

The flint tower of the church was originally topped by a spire which became unstable in the 1830s and had to be replaced by a brick superstructure. This in its turn was shaken by an earth tremor in 1884, and by 1963 was in such dangerous condition that the decision was taken to demolish it and build a replica of the original spire.

Far mightier is the church of Stoke-by-Nayland, riding the wave-crest of its ridge like a great galleon. Utterly different from Dedham church, it was almost as great a favourite with Constable. The massively buttressed tower is of flint and red brick, rising in five slightly contracting stages 120 feet to crocketed pinnacles recognizable from miles around. Within the south chapel are brasses and other memorials to a number of distinguished families, including the Howards and Tendrings, whose impaled arms appear on the font and in other parts of the church. The Lady Katherine Howard commemorated in the brass near the east window of the chapel became great-grandmother of Anne Boleyn and Catherine Howard, and so of two queens of England. Thomas Howard of Tendring Hall became in due course second Duke of Norfolk, having commanded the archers at Bosworth Field and later the English army at Flodden.

The village is well designed for the stroller. Its four main streets form the four sides of a near square. From the summit of the steep climb out of the Stour valley one can saunter past timbered buildings —those nearest the church being in a somewhat sorry state—past the school, sharp right towards the junction with Polstead Street and the steep lane to Polstead itself, and sharp right again along the trim shopping street to the nice crossroads cluster of inns and brightly plastered houses. The last right turn completes the square, opening out on to the broad approach to the church.

North-west lies Lavenham, a radiant survival of the Middle Ages with a stooping, lurching family of timbered and colour-washed houses and cottages climbing up one slope only to totter down another. Its great Guildhall is a sumptuous spread of timber, recalling the days of the weavers who made Lavenham blue cloth famous all over Europe. When trade declined, the building was for a time a prison, of which the reformer John Howard wrote:

> Prisoners always kept indoors: the court not secure: no water: no straw, no proper separation of female prisoners. Employment, spinning wool.

So even in the late eighteenth century the skills and tasks known to most men were still those of the wool trade! It had been a very different picture three hundred years earlier. At the end of the Wars of the Roses, Thomas Spring 'the Rich Clothier' was indeed rich enough to play a major part with the thirteenth Earl of Oxford in building Lavenham's wonderful parish church of SS Peter and Paul. He did not live to see the completion of the 141-foot tower, work on which was several times delayed until other clothiers donated or bequeathed money for it. Even now, overpowering as it is, the tower is not as originally planned: it should have had battlements and turrets, and even the holes for the scaffolding were not made good until 1909. But it is still a noble achievement, and Thomas Spring deserves to lie at peace in the chapel he built for himself and his wife within the church.

A book of engravings of the church was published by Isaac Taylor, who lived and worked at Shilling Grange in Shilling Street between 1786 and 1796. He is less well remembered, though, than his daughter Jane, who wrote 'Twinkle, twinkle, little star'. The name of Shilling Street has nothing to do with currency matters: there was no mint here, or anything of that kind; it is a corruption of Schylling, one of the Flemings who settled here to teach and practise the weaving craft.

An old Wool Hall has been incorporated into the *Swan* inn, as indeed have many lesser edifices over the years. More recent history is preserved behind a glass panel on the wall of the bar: part of the counter on which American servicemen from Second World War air bases scrawled and incised their signatures.

The running water needed in the cloth manufactories, large or small, still runs—or ambles—not merely through Kersey but right across its main street. This is truly a street village: from either end one approaches by means of a sharp bend and a downward plunge to and through the watersplash, followed by a climb to another bend. From either direction Kersey is invisible, apart from the top of its church tower, until one is actually upon it. The lovely shock of first seeing it can never be repeated; but I still approach with pleasureable anticipation and pretend that I don't know what's waiting for me round the corner.

A few attractive houses are tucked away into little lanes opening off the southern slope, but most of what Kersey has to offer is plain to see in its main thoroughfare. A horse's tail, once the trade insignia of a veterinary surgeon, dangles from the corner of a house near the ford. The brightness of one side of the street can distract attention from the darkly mellowed brick of a Tudor house adjoining the footbridge over the ford. The little gardens climbing up both sides of the cleft are trim and appealing at most seasons of the year.

Yet still I have a softer spot for Chelsworth, a few miles down the road from here. It has no pretensions, no tea-shoppe, no brisk trade in picture postcards. But it has a perky little double-humped bridge, an unkempt pond, very well-kempt houses predominantly of timber, plaster and thatch; and it is a village where people live—just that.

Visitors to Suffolk think first of the cluster of wool towns and villages, Constable country, or the east coast resorts. But whatever the fluctuations of industry, commerce, fishing and coastal traffic, the county's agriculture has continued from sheer necessity, and the hardest working villages are often to be found strung out along roads crossing the wide farmlands. Some are at the meeting-place of three or four roads, serving a widely scattered community.

Coddenham has hidden itself away as if to avoid commitment to anyone in particular. It is close to Ipswich, but not too close. The Romans were here, but have left little mark. There is a medieval farm, a park—and once there were any number of pubs, now turned into private houses but remembered locally as the *Griffon* (later the *Crown*), the *Live and Let Live*, and the mercifully surviving *Duke's Head*. The peer in question was John Dudley, Duke of Northumberland, who tried to put his daughter-in-law, Lady Jane Grey, on the throne of England in order to thwart the Catholic Mary. The people of East Anglia, however, rallied to Mary when she raised her standard at Framlingham Castle, and Northumberland ended up on the block in 1553. One road narrows disconcertingly on its way towards Pettaugh and the wide tractor-ridden prairies of High Suffolk beyond; another seeks out a Roman road leading to more farming hamlets; and another joins the main road to Ipswich through Claydon. In the middle of all this, somewhere unspecific yet real and identifiable through a glimpse here, a fleeting intimation there, is one of the most famous villages in the county—a fictitious one. People who have never heard of Akenham and Charsfield will have heard of

Akenfield, the composite picture of a rural community so unforgettably depicted by Ronald Blythe in his book which I have defined as fiction while knowing all along that it is true in a way few demonstrably 'factual' books are true.

A more recent publication dealing with a real-life incident in the real Akenham tells, in fact, a more outrageous story about more incredible characters than Mr Blythe, one feels, would have dared to introduce into his own poetic semi-reportage. And the story of its inception is a fascinating little tale in itself, showing, not for the first time, how much we need diligent historians and our own unremitting curiosity if we are to fit the formative influences, freaks, conflicts and parochial dramas of the past into the pattern of our own village as we know it today. One man finds a forgotten prehistoric or Roman trackway; another a priest's hole; another the verbal corruption of an ancient name which suddenly makes sense. Ronald Fletcher, a Yorkshireman, stumbled across some pages of nineteenth-century Suffolk village history in a small Suffolk town, and pursued the overgrown track through contemporary newspaper files until he was in a position to edit the accumulated material into a coherent picture of not just a village scandal but of something which at that time perplexed and divided the whole country. *The Akenham Burial Case*, published by Wildwood House in 1974, tells how the burial of a rural labourer's child led to a sweeping change in a national institution. There is no real question here of some dauntless village Hampden; but one may feel that both Hampden and Thomas Gray would, if watching, have been agog to learn of the outcome.

On an August afternoon in 1878 the corpse of two-year-old Joseph Ramsey was brought for burial to Akenham parish churchyard, whose pastor was also rector of Claydon. The Rev. George Drury was waiting to receive the coffin, but made it clear that as the child was the son of Baptist parents and had therefore not been baptized in infancy, he was entitled neither to interment in consecrated ground nor to the reading of a Christian burial service. The Rev. Wickham Tozer, minister of a Congregational church in Ipswich, who had accompanied the parents, began to read a service over the child outside the churchyard. At this the rector, it was shortly alleged in a news item in the *East Anglian Daily Times*, told the parents to hurry up and bury their dead child and have whatever service they chose afterwards. When asked to be quiet and allow Mr Tozer to continue, he declared 'it is wrong to perform funeral rites of a Christian form over the remains of an unbaptized child'. It was intimated in the press report that at one stage the rival clergymen nearly came to blows.

Unfortunately when the story was taken up by other newspapers and, goaded by criticism of his callousness, the Rev. Drury sued for libel, it turned out that the account of the event had been written by one of the main participants, Mr Tozer.

During the trial the public learned that Mr Drury, who liked to be referred to as Father Drury, had been known to denounce Protestantism in scathing terms, maintained a small nunnery in the spacious gardens of his rectory, and had been involved with the strange Father Ignatius in his attempts to revive monasticism within the Church of England. He had been in trouble previously on a charge of keeping a young woman in the nunnery against her will, and had been fined for striking a labourer with a red-hot poker after the man had shouted 'No Popery' at him. At the time of the Akenham incident he was under monition from his bishop on counts concerning the display and use of 'certain articles and ornaments'. Mr Tozer, on the other hand, appeared to be a bit of a firebrand whose motives aroused the suspicions of a rival newspaper:

> What is to be said of the article which he drew up for the *East Anglian Times*, carefully speaking of himself in the third person, as if it proceeded from an admiring but impartial reporter, introducing statements which appear questionable in point of fact, and dragging in irrelevant matters, simply to excite odium against Mr Drury and the Church to which he belongs? It is too obvious to be denied that its main object was to make capital for the cause of political Dissent, and especially on the burials question.

The burials question was at the root of the whole scandal. Although every citizen had the right of burial in his parish churchyard, that churchyard was firmly under the sole jurisdiction of the Church of England and a burial service could be read only if the body was that of a person baptized according to that Church's tenets. The expense of providing separate Nonconformist burial grounds meant that they were few and far between, and in most parts of the country outside large towns there were no such things as locally maintained non-denominational or inter-denominational cemeteries. Dissenters and other reformers had for a long time been clamouring for a new approach to the vexed problem, but were persistently blocked by Anglican interests in Parliament.

The jury found for the Rev. George Drury in his action against the editor of the *East Anglian Daily Times* but awarded him only a contemptuous forty shillings damages. Press comment flared up again, and although a few papers and correspondents denounced the 'parson baiting' in which Tozer and others were said to have indulged, the general reaction was one of disgust at the rector's lack of Christian charity in the presence of bereaved parents. A national subscription raised money to defray the editor's legal costs; and the editor himself helped to provide a fitting tombstone for little Joseph Ramsey. Most important of all, ammunition was supplied to the promoters of the Burial Laws Amendment Act which, after years of frustration, reached the statute book in 1880.

Claydon Rectory has become a private residence, but still has the high wall which Drury erected to keep at bay those parishioners who yelled 'Papist' and threw stones into his garden, and the mock ruins which he constructed to suit his odd, romantic tastes. Lime Kiln Cottage in the village was once the home of Countess Sophie Benckendorff, widow of a Russian ambassador. At the moment it is owned by a former secretary of the Royal Academy who has used its gardens to grow what may well be the largest collection of old hybrid perpetual roses in England—including the Countess's namesake, Sophie's Perpetual.

Village churches across the county and some little way into Norfolk display varyingly ornate porches, walls and buttresses of flushwork: patterns of intermingled freestone and knapped flint, at its best in Long Melford but splendid, too, at Blythburgh and many another unexpected corner. In the Waveney valley there is a proliferation of round-towered churches, most of them conceived as refuges from Danish raiders, with doors well above ground level through which a ladder could be hauled once the populace had been safely gathered in. It is a fertile valley, and to the north the ground is so rich that every square inch of it is greedily exploited: hedges are torn down to open up wider and wider expanses to the plough, and some villages are little more than isolated work camps for the farm employees.

On a Monday morning late in April 1772, according to a newspaper of the time,

> a number of rioters to the amount of 60 passed through the town of New Buckenham with a horse's tassel fixed to the top of a pole by way of a standard, and horns blowing in order to join a number of the like sort assembled at Carlton and Bunwell, when they proceeded to visit several of the farmers in the neighbourhood, from whom they extorted meat, beer, etc. In their march through Buckenham they threatened the town with a visit in the afternoon. The principal inhabitants immediately assembling together invited several of the farmers in Old Buckenham and Barham to their assistance, in order, if possible, to persuade them to disperse, or if lenient measures would not do, to protect their houses from being plundered by force. While they were waiting, in expectation of the rioters entering the town of New Buckenham, a person sent to watch their motions arrived with the information that the mob was passing over Barham heath by the side of the town of New Buckenham for Mr Chenery's baking house at Barham upon which it was agreed immediately to pursue them, and some on horseback, others on foot armed with clubs came up with them, and after a short parley they knocked down the standard bearer and soon dispersed the rest.... Many of the rioters who were committed to the house of correction at Chelmsford, were ordered at the quarter sessions there to be removed from the jail, to take their trial at the next assizes: they are all heavily ironed. Warrants are issued out against the ringleaders, many of whom are daily committed.

The cause of all this was the rising price of corn and a scarcity brought about by speculative hoarding. When it was discovered that corn was being shipped out of the country to make high profits in France while the English poor were close to starvation, there were food riots throughout the region, and indignant bands of labourers tried to force grocers and butchers to sell to them at what they considered reasonable prices. In some districts troops were called in to quell the disturbances.

New Buckenham today is no more a 'town' than it was then: its population is not much more than four hundred. It did, however, have an important market-place, in which the polygonal seventeenth-century market-house stands on stilts, with an old whipping-post at the centre, at which some of the arrested demonstrators probably suffered. There are traces of an unusual circular Norman keep on a moated mound, and a small building which used to be its chapel.

Moving across Norfolk towards Sandringham and the north-west coastal resorts, we notice a toffee-coloured stone in many village walls which gives them, at a distance, a soft effect: at times it looks like slightly rubbed-up velvet, and from the corner of one's eye can seem oddly out of focus. Studied more closely, this carstone proves to be anything but velvety. The men who dug it from Snettisham quarry and those who had to build with it found its fractured edges cruelly sharp. It can be found in thin brick form like slabs of chocolate, but splits easily and often had to be used in irregular chips packed together.

At Houghton is another of those villages moved bodily into a new situation by a great landowner wishing to extend his park. The deferential little avenue of sentinel cottages outside the iron gates of the hall dates from 1729. The church is not with them but inside the park, and is the resting place of the man for whom the house was built—Sir Robert Walpole, born in Houghton and always protesting, even in the middle of his most cunning ministerial manoeuvres, that he was basically a simple Norfolk farmer, happier on his own soil than wrestling with the complexities of metropolitan and political intrigue.

As a farmer Walpole was not, however, in the same class as a Member of Parliament for Norfolk whose estate lay some miles further north, at Holkham. Thomas William Coke, created Earl of Leicester in 1837, transformed the face of the saltings and impoverished soil in his ownership—on all of which, Lady Townshend had declared, 'all you will see will be one blade of grass, and two rabbits fighting for that'—into fertile farmland whose reputation spread far beyond Holkham. It all began when one of his tenant farmers refused to renew a lease on the grounds that an increase from three shillings and six pence a year to five shillings a year was unreasonable, considering the poor condition of the land. Coke, though heavily committed to parliamentary duties and to other administrative matters on his large estate, decided that the answer was to farm his land himself. He discussed agricultural matters with other local farmers, and then went further afield for scientific advice. Instead of growing three crops in succession, he grew two and turned the land over to pasture for two years. Most significantly of all, he realized the value of digging marl from deep pits and spreading it over the sandy, flinty surface. After consultation with the famous Leicestershire cattle breeder, Robert Bakewell, he expanded his herds and flocks, not only for their milk and meat potential but because of the way they could enrich the soil: 'Muck is the mother of money', as the old Norfolk proverb has it. Soon tenant farmers were willing to pay vastly increased rents for the privilege of working such land, especially as Coke was prepared to grant long leases to men whom he could trust to follow his methods. Unusually for that era, he refused ever to enforce, directly or by insinuation, his own political views on his tenants and workers or to take for granted their electoral support. It was reported that he was a bit of a tartar on religious matters, insisting that the villagers should attend church regularly and be seen to attend church; but at the same time he was unstintingly generous in the help he gave towards their children's education and towards their living conditions. And he was not by any means a puritan. His biographer, A. M. W. Stirling, records that although guests were expected to finish the day with evening prayers, servants were tactfully provided to catch them as they fell over in the middle of their devotions as a result of the wine so liberally poured by their host.

'Coke of Norfolk' will not be forgotten in Holkham. His descendants still live at the hall, a yellow Palladian building open to the public on certain afternoons during the summer, its main approach between Lady Leicester's terraced almshouses leading through a gateway past a long lake which was once an inlet from the sea, with a working pottery and a garden centre specializing in alpine plants and shrubs.

Even Coke would have blenched at the prospect of trying to reclaim Breckland by the methods he used at Holkham. This freakish steppeland, sprawling across the border of Norfolk and Suffolk on either side of the Little Ouse, consists at present of conifer forests, military airfields, and battle training grounds. Before the spread of the plantations its sandy topsoil could be blown in such great drifts that one farmer, asked which county his farm was in, replied: 'That do depend which way the wind's a-blowin'!'

Santon Downham, on an attractive stretch of the Little Ouse, is the district headquarters of the Forestry Commission in Thetford Chase. They have laid out a two-mile forest trail through the broadleaf woods near what is left of the old village, the 1969 plantation commemorating the Commission's first fifty years, and other interesting aspects of arboricultural work. The lime avenue leading back to the village is particularly glorious: its first trees were planted in 1880, and the whole gleaming length of it is maintained by felling and replanting short sections every ten years or so. In addition to this well-marked walk there are riverside paths, a bridge over the stream, and on the northern bank a near-derelict little church which, like the few struggling farms in the district, was more than once almost inundated by sandstorms. The modern village is made up of quite stylish bungalows for forestry workers: with their technical know-how, and all the equipment at their disposal, it is hardly surprising that the church by the village green looks so much neater, its graveyard so much better kept, than its neglected sister across the river. Like many Breckland villages, it lacks a pub.

In Neolithic times this apparent wasteland was one of the most

densely populated areas of England. There are tumuli everywhere,
hundreds of indications of prehistoric settlements, and even today a
walk across the heath or along one of the nature reserve paths may
very easily produce a number of flint tools or arrow heads. The dips
and hillocks of Grime's Graves, a mile or so from Santon Downham,
were once thought to be the configurations of a Saxon or Danish encampment; then, as superficial research showed them to be older, it
was surmised that this might have been an Iceni village; and at last
a clerical archaeologist, Canon Greenwell, began more vigorous
excavations and revealed deep flint mines and a network of tunnels
unquestionably going back some three thousand years. Through
1973 and 1974 a wide tract has been roofed in while modern excavations are carried on which, it is believed, should uncover even more
extensive workings than those already discovered.

Later races did not find the scrubland so congenial. The Romans
were certainly here, but most of their relics have been found around
the fringes, as with the Mildenhall treasure, or along the strategic
track of the Peddars' Way. Most surviving village sites, as the late
W. G. Clarke pointed out in his classic *In Breckland Wilds*, appear
to have been established by the Saxons: thirteen parish names end
in *ton* and two in *tone*, twenty in *ham*, and a fair proportion of
others in *ing*, *well*, *wold*, *den*, *toft*, *don* and *ey*. But farming here
was always a battle. 'Fit only for rabbits and rye', it has been said
of the soil. In and around Breckland there are about thirty identifiable deserted village sites, most of them having given up the ghost
between the middle of the fifteenth and the end of the sixteenth
centuries. And this in a region which by then was not supporting a
very large population anyway. Today, in spite of industrial development around Thetford and the employment offered in the region of
air force and army installations, it is one of the most sparsely populated areas in the kingdom. The army, ironically, has done much to
preserve the original heathland character against the encroachments
of the Forestry Commission's conifers; but has done some destruction of its own. On the ordnance maps, some minor roads come to
an abrupt halt, and dotted lines imply that only impassable trackways remain. In reality, many of these roads continue: you will

come to the junction and find an old signpost there, with the name of a village or hamlet upon it . . . and, below, a War Department or Ministry of Defence or similarly phrased warning that there is no thoroughfare. Sometimes armoured cars appear. Along a permitted road there will be red signs forbidding you to park and strike out across scrubland: unexploded shells await you. Within one set of gates, often left open and unguarded, I once found the splintered skeleton of a half-timbered farmhouse and the phantom of a village street, shot to pieces by its fellow countrymen.

Wooden construction was rare in the east coast counties after 1604, when rapid consumption of timber and the difficulty of growing new woodlands in these climatic conditions led to a royal proclamation decreeing the use of brick and stone in future new houses. When existing wooden framing or window frames were in need of repair, they should wherever possible be replaced by brick or stone. Old stud cottages gave way to the flinty, ageless buildings we associate with Breckland, their starkness leavened here and there by imaginative patterning of the natural or knapped flints themselves or by use of brick corners, sills and lintels, and by galleting—setting chips of brick, flint, tile, carstone or even cinders into the mortar.

On the Peddars' Way where it enters the northernmost brecks, now subdued and made green by intensive farming, stands the walled village of Castle Acre. It is best approached from the Swaffham to Fakenham road, by a hill which steepens and narrows through the thirteenth-century gateway into the village square, enclosed within the remains of the large bailey. There were once extensive Roman earthworks here, on which the Normans superimposed their motte and bailey, with a massive shell keep. The village houses, shops and inns fit tidily into the layout of the old fortifications. Spread out across the greensward below are the ruins of a great Cluniac priory, established by one of the Warenne family who were also responsible for the castle. Entered through a fine Tudor gatehouse, it retains the beautiful outline of its west front and a fair amount of the prior's lodging. At one time a farmhouse was built into the ruins, but this has been picked out again.

Lakenheath is a village with several conflicting allegiances. Its

22 *Shottery, Warwickshire*

interminable main street goes on for so long that one could almost fancy oneself travelling above an old railway track, and for once the modern brick villas come as a relief—in all that original flint. The wonderful church seems far too rich for its setting. The original Saxon foundation was given to St Etheldreda, but its real treasures are of later date: there is a fine Norman chancel arch, and angels with agitated wings stare out from faces mutilated by the Cromwellians over a motley collection of twisting, glistening beasts on the bench-ends below.

Behind the village, the American air base is a far larger township. Beside it runs one of the best remaining examples of the original heathland, the breck on whose western rim Lakenheath stands. But the village name can be misleading: its 'heath' was once 'hythe', the Old English word used along the coast, along rivers, and in the fenlands to define a landing place. For with one side of its street virtually defining the western edge of Breckland, it looks from the other side out on to the Fens.

Although the Romans and their successors made repeated attempts to reclaim the swamp and marshland formed in this silted bay of the North Sea, it was not until the seventeenth century that real progress was made. The fourth Earl of Bedford, after whom Bedford Level is named, and his mercantile 'Adventurers' whose name is preserved in Adventurers' Fen engaged the Dutch engineer Cornelius Vermuyden to straighten out the wandering, flooding streams and sluice them against tidal inflow. Lock gates and embankments were persistently destroyed by local folk who feared their livelihood from fishing and wildfowling would be jeopardized; but these 'Fenland Tigers' failed, and firm, fertile land was won from the bog.

Existing settlements could expand with less fear of inundation. New villages owed their situation and trade more to the interlocking of drainage channels and the solidly embanked rivers than to roadways. Their names explain their situation: *lode* is a navigable cut; *drove* a cut with a path along its bank; *hythe* a quay, or landing place; and *mere* a stretch of farmland which was once a lake. Apart from Ely's town and superb cathedral, some monastic ruins and a few churches, the Fens have little to offer in the way of architectural

23 *Staithes, Yorkshire*

treasure. The great forests whose remnants often come to the surface as warped, iron-hard 'bog oak' were choked thousands of years ago by the formation of peat, so that workable timber has always been hard to come by. With no local building stone, either, the region has had to rely mainly on manufactured materials such as brick and tile.

What the villages lack in picturesque buildings, they often make up for in their fascinating integration with the surrounding country-side. Reach Lode is an historic feature of the village of Reach where a Roman canal joins the River Cam. By the early Middle Ages the place had become the main river port for Cambridge, and the banks of the hythe would have been as busy as those of Fordwich, in a similar position *vis-à-vis* Canterbury. Like Fordwich, Reach has now dwindled to a village, still with its village green on which Reach Fair was inaugurated in the time of Henry I.

Still closer to Cambridge, along the edge of Swaffham Prior Fen, we come to the neighbouring Swaffhams—Prior and Bulbeck. Swaffham Prior's houses are too close to their twisting main street, but several of them have a most unusual view on the other side of that street. In one churchyard are two churches, one of them with a double dedication: it is the only known English partner of that Devonian St Cyriac (or Cyricus) and St Julitta. Its neighbour, St Mary's, is the older, having been founded early in the twelfth century. A hundred years or so later, St Cyriac and Julitta was built as a separate parish church. The two were united in 1667 and continued to function in tandem until in 1787 St Mary's tower was struck by lightning and the spire fell into the nave. The sensible thing seemed to be to renovate St Cyriac with material from the damaged church of St Mary, and early in the nineteenth century one might have expected the restorations to result in the survival of St Cyriac and the gradual decline of St Mary. In fact, work on St Cyriac was shoddily executed, while restoration of part of St Mary's by a local family kept that building in reasonable trim. Now it is St Mary's which serves as parish church, while the other church turns into a ragged Gothick-romantic ruin.

Earith stands on the county boundary between the shires of Cambridge and Huntingdon. More significantly, it stands at one of Vermuyden's great junctions, where the Old Bedford River and the New Bedford River (or Hundred Foot Drain, as it is poetically called) meet the Great Ouse. Between the two parallel arteries lies an old Roman encampment known as The Bulwark, which was strengthened during the Civil War by the Parliamentarians. We are, after all, now in Oliver Cromwell's own county.

The hamlets of Wood Walton and Holme are jammed, a few miles apart, right against the main railway line from Peterborough to London; but they have in common something much older and more fundamental than the iron road. Near Wood Walton are both the Wood Walton Fen Nature Reserve and the Monks Wood Nature Reserve and experimental station, where agriculture and such thorny problems as pesticides and pollution are studied; and near Holme is the Holme Fen Nature Reserve, incorporating what is thought to be the lowest-lying land in England, some ten feet below sea level and sagging slightly every year—as one can see from the gradual emergence of a steel post driven into the ground many years ago.

But Cambridgeshire, Huntingdonshire and Lincolnshire are not all reclaimed swampland. South of Cambridge are two quite different villages. Grantchester can be reached from the city by punt or skiff, or by a most agreeable stroll across the fields. Somewhat congested by undergraduates during term-time and by tourists during the holiday season, it still manages to preserve its slightly self-conscious charm, with thatched cottages, sociable inns, and the vicarage where Rupert Brooke lived for a time and wrote before his death in the First World War. Beside the road to Trumpington lies the shaded mere of Byron's Pool, a tranquil spot frequented by many poets other than Byron. A stretch of Trumpington village suffers from the traffic of the A10, but it keeps its quiet backwaters to itself. In the church is the second oldest brass in England, and one of the most splendid, though it often proves difficult to study: assiduous brass-rubbers are for ever at work upon Sir Roger de Trumpington, who nevertheless remains in splendid condition. The village cross is the work of Eric Gill.

At nearby Sawston the first of the Cambridgeshire Village Colleges, imaginative pioneer experiment in further education, was opened in 1930. A later one at Soham stages a festival every May with lectures, discussions, local exhibitions, music and dancing.

Off the main road from Cambridge to Huntingdon lie, on a twisting, fissured stretch of the Great Ouse, the two Hemingfords. In ancient times there was the ford of the Hemings here. Hemingford Abbots once belonged to Ramsey Abbey. Its timbered, thatched, colour-washed houses stand at all angles, with a few modern intrusions, along the road into Hemingford Grey, which always looks as if it intends to win every possible award for the best-kept village anywhere. Its Norman manor is the oldest inhabited house in the country, set within a square moat whose fourth side, reached by beautiful gardens, is the river itself. The hall of the house is on the upper floor, with a doorway which must have been reached by an external stairway. One side road in the village comes to a delightful dead end against the river, and offers a boat-bedecked view of the water curving round beneath St James's church. The church tower carries the stump of a spire, now crowned by eight stone balls, which is all that remains of the spire blown into the river in 1741. The pieces are believed to be still lying in the mud of the river bed.

The hamlet of Little Gidding is, as we have noted earlier, a companion piece to T. S. Eliot's East Coker. It consists of little more than a cluster of cottages, a farmhouse, and the parish church of St John the Evangelist. The church is reached by a path through the farmyard and across a field, and the path is much used: this is a place of pilgrimage.

Set fair and square before the west door is the tombstone of Nicholas Ferrar, in appearance and associations more like an altar than a grave. Son of a well-to-do London merchant, and by his late twenties a figure of some consequence in the Virginia Company, Nicholas became a Member of Parliament in 1624. But then he decided to turn his back on the affairs of the world and dedicate himself to a life of religious meditation and good works. With his mother, and brother and sister and their families, he settled at Little Gidding and rebuilt the manor house and church. Word of his piety and his charitable ideals began to spread, and in 1633 Charles I paid a respectful visit to the community. This did the Ferrars no good. Nicholas died a few years later, but his brother was put in the invidious position of having to offer Charles a hiding-place in 1646, word of which reached the Roundheads, who sacked the house and church. The church was rebuilt in the eighteenth century and has been well cared for ever since. In 1946 the Society of the Friends of Little Gidding was formed to perpetuate Nicholas Ferrar's ideals and to organize an annual pilgrimage, which takes place on the second Saturday in July.

About a third of the village names in Lincolnshire end in -*by*, a reminder of the years of the Danelaw. The Danes must have found the shallow coastline and the bleak levels so reminiscent of their own Jutland that one wonders why they bothered to settle at all. Part of the county overlaps the Fens, but the littoral is marshland rather than fen, intersected by dykes which feed North Sea salt into the ground. In the vast open fields, squat hamlets appear from a distance as no more than glorified farmsteads; and this is in effect what many of them are.

Windmills were among the few lofty features of the landscape, as much for drainage as for grinding corn, and there are still a fair number to be seen. At Burgh-le-Marsh, raised on a humped island above the Lindsey plain known as Middle Marsh, a tower mill is maintained in working order. It has four floors open to the public, and a building beside it has been adopted by a local school as a windmill museum, with models, maps and photographs. Burgh itself has been here a long time. A Bronze Age axe-head was unearthed from a chicken run by a local antiquary, and there is an Anglo-Saxon burial mound called Cock or Cockpit Hill.

To the west another hulking tower thrusts up against the sky. This is the huge keep of Tattershall Castle, dwarfing the village which expanded in Tudor times to serve it. It was built by Lord Cromwell in handsome red brick within a moat as devious as many a marshland waterway. Although it looks a massive and defiant fortress it was designed primarily as a dwelling, and a well-appointed one at that. There are glazed windows instead of defensive slits, each carrying the arms of some subsequent owner. The Gothic stone fireplaces are finely carved, and there is elaborate heraldic vaulting. From the battlements one can survey a great uninterrupted panorama of countryside, taking in Lincoln Cathedral, Boston Stump, and the village attractively spread out below. In the churchyard is a row of almshouses, and behind the market-place the remains of a choir school also founded by the Lord Treasurer. He is commemorated within the cruciform collegiate church by a headless brass, and brasses to other members of the family are displayed in a brightness of light through huge, clear windows.

We owe the preservation of Tattershall, as we do the much-visited castle at Bodiam, to Lord Curzon. He saved it from dereliction before the First World War, and recovered the fireplaces which had been dismantled for sale to America; and in 1926 it came under the terms of his will to the National Trust.

But the most endearing villages in Lincolnshire are those of the Wolds. Because of the general flatness of the region, these uplands seem quite imposing as one approaches, but nowhere reach more than five hundred feet. Every little gap and gully seems to shelter a little red-brick settlement snuggled around its stumpy church. There are Croxby, Clixby and an assortment of Claxbys. And there are two Bolingbrokes. New Bolingbroke is a calculated model village from the early nineteenth century. Old Bolingbroke goes back a lot further: John of Gaunt held the castle here, and it was the birthplace of his son who became Henry IV. During the Civil War it was a Royalist stronghold until Fairfax crossed the Humber with his cavalry and added them to Cromwell's forces, which then routed the numerically superior Royalist cavalry at Winceby. The Parliamentarians pulled down part of the castle and left the rest to decay. All that is visible today is an uneven pattern of mounds. John of Gaunt's church still stands, though somewhat restored and disfigured.

In another gentle cleft of the chalk Wolds, not far from Horncastle, is Tennyson's birthplace, Somersby. The Rev. George Tennyson, became incumbent in 1806, and Alfred, the rector's fourth child, was born in 1809. The Georgian rectory is still there, facing the church. When the boy was seven he was sent to stay with his grandmother in Louth, and went to the grammar school there for a while, but returned home in 1820 and continued his education under his father. When the Rev. George died in 1831, the new rector allowed the family to stay on in their home for a further five or six years, after which they moved to Essex. There are several Tennyson memorials in the church, including a bust of the poet.

In his *Ode to Memory*, Tennyson invokes—at a rather early age for nostalgia—the ambience of his childhood:

> *Pour round mine ears the livelong bleat*
> *Of the thick-fleeced sheep from wattled folds*
>   *Upon the ridged wolds,*
> *When the first matin-song hath waken'd loud*
> *Over the dark dewy earth forlorn,*
> *What time the amber morn*
> *Forth gushes from beneath a low-hung cloud.*

CHAPTER SIX

The Heartlands

What is so important about Puckeridge? To most of the counties north of London it would seem to be a lodestar. On every trunk road there is some branch indicated on one of those vast signboards; or, if you are actually on the A10, there are encouraging signs to assure you that you have really and truly hit the right road at last and will soon be there. It must at the very least be a major crossroads linking north and south, east and west—some historic 'spaghetti junction' on which the major thoroughfares of the eastern counties converge. I have been surprised by its name appearing suddenly on some turn-off in Suffolk, or beside a secondary road in Essex. In Hertfordshire one might be forgiven for supposing it to be the county town.

Yet in reality it proves to be a dusty thoroughfare village sprouting a main road to Bishop's Stortford and a B road towards Cambridge which dutifully rejoins the awful A10 before entering the city. I would dearly love to know the grounds on which some route strategist decided to make this unassuming, wounded little place a key reference point on his maps and his great turn-off signs.

I have called Puckeridge dusty and wounded. I'd like to think that these adjectives were already out of date. When, a few years ago, I had to drive to and from London twice each week, I used the road through Barley and Barkway into the exhaust-smelling, smeared bottleneck of Puckeridge and found time—only just—to see that its houses were, beneath the layer of grime, at best distinguished and at worst trim and attractive. Near the tight, perilous junction was an inn with a spacious car park, a sparkling frontage, and that indefinable air of hospitality which the connoisseur of licensed premises recognizes at once by some magic involving the hang of a door, the colour of a beam, or the flowers in a window-box. But to *stop* in Puckeridge . . .? Not then. Last time I took that route, on the outward journey from London, I nearly missed the village altogether. The A10 has been diverted around it, and now the village street, dusting itself off, is readjusting to the notion of being a village street once more. Saved from being shaken to pieces, will it now die of sheer quietude? Will passing traffic utterly by-pass and bankrupt the inn? If all goes well, the sequel should be just the opposite. For centuries the great coaching road to Yarmouth ran through the village of Stratford St Mary. When in our own time it was by-passed by the dual carriageway of the A12, a slump might reasonably have been forecast in the fortunes of local innkeepers. Instead, the village has perceptibly brightened and the inns have profited. I shall have another look at Puckeridge very soon. When so many villages are being debauched, swallowed up by towns, or shouldered aside by some brutal road development, it is good to know that others are being granted a new lease of life.

Of Barley and Barkway, along that undulating back road, perhaps the less said the better. The route should never be one for lorries or for holidaymakers seeking a short cut. Yet it was beside this road that the forerunners of the modern metal plaques directing us this way and that way originated. Trinity Hall, Cambridge, set up at Trumpington the first milestone in a sequence ending at Barkway in 1727, the earliest known regular use of milestones. Barkway's leisurely, winding main street is a gentle slope of mellow red brick which deserves more than a casually approving turn of the head. When it has left the village behind, the street somehow never becomes an independent road but continues its curves, its rises and falls, as if thinking things over before greeting another splash of houses on the slope of Barley—this time with some nice thatch and plaster, a bit of pargeting, and even some weather-boarding. The village inn was once burnt down but rebuilt on a corner, where the 'gallows' sign of the *Fox and Hounds* spans a side road, pictorially commemorating the occasion when a fox took refuge in the inn from hounds and huntsmen.

The cherished river of a neighbouring county rises in Hertfordshire. The rector of Ashwell church claims, indeed, that the spring of the Rhee, which blossoms into the Cam, is actually in his rectory garden; and once told me of one of his sons, when a boy chorister at King's College, furiously telling a bullying colleague that if he wanted to he could stop all training for the Boat Race. Ashwell takes its name from this source, surrounded as it is by ash trees. Outside the village is an Iron Age fort, and traces of a Roman road: the lay-out of the village, unlike so many later settlements, follows the original Roman pattern fairly closely. The pargeting of some of the seventeenth-century houses is as lavish as one can find anywhere in East Anglia—in some cases, in deep relief fit to compare with ex-amples in Clare, Hadleigh and Ipswich. The church is largely four-teenth century, and into the base of its tower is incised a unique contemporary representation of Old St Paul's Cathedral as it was before the Great Fire. An old timbered Tythe House has been restored and made into a museum of Ashwell's distant and more recent past.

Hertfordshire has suffered from the appetite of the Great Wen just as Kent, Surrey, Bucks and Berks have suffered. Escape to the north or south takes many miles; along the Thames to the east is almost impossible; and to the west . . .?

During a statistical survey of Home Counties villages carried out a year or two back for administrative purposes, it was stipulated that a 'village' should be taken to mean a community of not more than two thousand people, of whom not less than thirty per cent should be engaged in remunerative work solely within that community. On these terms, there proved to be only seven true villages in the region. Places which prided themselves on being villages were dormitory towns; and the villagers were London-orientated commuters. But in their defence one can plead that, whatever the recent growth of population and in spite of a surface rash of bungalows and stockbroker-Tudor mansions, the original nucleus pulses strongly in the centre of it all.

Nobody, for example, could think of Stoke Poges as anything other than a village even though its population is well over the four thousand mark. Its churchyard, seen as inevitably through the lych-gate as Dedham Vale will for ever be seen through Constable's eyes, is not just a country churchyard but *the* country churchyard. Thomas Gray's *Elegy* was never specifically associated with Stoke Poges by the poet himself; but no other place's claim is likely to be countenanced at this late date. Gray was born in London and came to the village with his mother only when he was twenty-five, after his father's death. They lived in a cottage on whose site Stoke Court was later built. The following year, 1742, he began to write the *Elegy in a Country Churchyard*, but clearly had difficulty in finishing it to his satisfaction: it was not done until 1750. Those who associate its composition with Stoke Poges claim that he used to sit under the yew tree still guarding the church porch.

Gray died in 1771 and was commemorated by an unobtrusive plaque in the church wall. But he was not to be allowed some quietly 'frail memorial' to implore 'the passing tribute of a sigh': in 1799 a huge monument designed by James Wyatt was set up in a thirteen-acre field beside the churchyard, thereafter known as Gray's Field.

Edging one's way out of the London sprawl by way of the Thames, one finds other villages swollen to riverside towns and anchorages; and here again, many of them guard jealously the last vestiges of their village character. At Laleham we meet another famous Thomas —Dr Arnold, who ran a small private school here before becoming head master of Rugby. His pupils must have been hard pressed, for Thomas Arnold taught fifty or sixty hours a week as well as writing voluminous treatises on a number of scholastic subjects. His son Matthew was born in 1822 in a house now demolished but marked by a cedar tree in what was once the Arnolds' garden. Matthew and other members of the family are buried in the churchyard. Laleham House, now a convent standing in grounds maintained by the local council as an open space, was once the home of the Earls of Lucan, one of whom is associated with the Charge of the Light Brigade.

Residents still speak of Cookham village, though it is difficult to give it the benefit of the doubt. But it is not so difficult to see what it once was. The village green, known as The Moor, is flanked by houses worthy of its spaciousness. Stanley Spencer was born in the house called Fernlea in Cookham High Street, and captured many aspects of the village, the towpath and the boat-house near the bridge which is the office of the Keeper of the Royal Swans.

Medmenham's *Dog and Badger* is a well-known inn, but possibly less well known than the architectural folly of Medmenham Abbey. This was built by the young eighteenth-century rake, Sir Francis

Dashwood, on the site of a ruined Cistercian monastery, for the use of his mock monastic fraternity. Dashwood and his drinking, whoring friends had been in the habit of meeting for childishly blasphemous rites in London and then on an island in the Thames near Hampton Court, but were anxious to have a more secluded clubhouse of their own. Sir Francis had an estate at West Wycombe, and only these few miles away at Medmenham he found the ideal spot. When he had done it up, it was still a ruin—a deliberately contrived, Gothick-romantic ruin. Here the brotherhood known as the Hell-Fire Club met, with all facilities for lavish orgies against a backdrop of pornographic frescoes. Unfortunately a book was written, apparently from information supplied by a renegade 'brother' or one in need of money, which brought sight-seeing crowds to Medmenham by the boat-load. Dashwood supplied new secret premises on his own estate at West Wycombe by having a system of caves dug into the hillside. It is recorded that the gardens of the house itself were laid out in such a way that from a high vantage point they presented the appearance of a naked woman.

Created Baron le Despencer, Dashwood went in for some more ecclesiastical restoration. He had the hilltop church rebuilt, and himself devised its interior more as a sitting-room than a place of worship. On the tower he set a huge hollow ball, within which as many as ten members of the Hell-Fire Club could squeeze at a time. He was eventually buried in a mausoleum at the east end.

The village of West Wycombe is largely in the hands of the National Trust. There are some lovely examples of houses from the fifteenth to the eighteenth century, saved from demolition or decay in 1929. Church Lane is entered through the picturesque archway of Church Loft, some four hundred years old. A timber and brick building, oversailing the pavement so far that one fears it will tilt out into the street, was once a rest-house for pilgrims.

It might have been expected that the earthbound ghosts of the Dashwood fraternity would haunt the scenes of their old debauches, but there are no stories of such apparitions. The fourteenth-century *George and Dragon* inn, however, has its own ghost. She once worked in the hostelry and, if she was as beautiful as legend tells, her presence must have been very good for trade. A visitor who stayed here at regular intervals—he sounds rather like an early commercial traveller—aroused the resentment of some younger locals who had their hearts set on the girl, and to get their own back they lured her to the celebrated caves by a message supposed to come from her mysterious admirer. The joke misfired. In a tussle the girl suffered a fractured skull and died that night in one of the rooms of the inn. Now, in the small hours, that same room will be suffused by a deathly chill, and she will set out to pace the corridor.

Upstream from Medmenham are Hambleden Lock and the hamlet of Mill End, linked by a combination bridge and footpath over the conflicting weirs into which canoeists throw themselves exuberantly. The watermill which gives the place its name dates from the fourteenth century, but there was a mill here long before that: one was recorded in Domesday Book as fetching an annual rent of £1. The present white-boarded mill has a turbine in place of the old waterwheel.

This is a good point of departure for an excursion via Hambleden into the Chilterns.

Beside the road from Mill End, remains of a Roman villa were found near Yewden Manor in 1911, with a mosaic floor and some touching personal ornaments—brooches, hairpins and a bracelet. The finds were displayed for a while in a little local museum, but have been transferred to the County Museum in Aylesbury. Near the lock is the Victorian brick and flint house of Greenlands, once the home of that W. H. Smith whose name is preserved on hundreds of bookshop frontages and who was created first Viscount Hambleden.

Hambleden has an admirable village green, with its complement of brick and flint cottages, a Georgian rectory, and a fourteenth-century church which has been described as a miniature cathedral. The oak altar in the nave carries the representation of a Cardinal's hat and Wolsey's arms, and may have been taken from a bed-head screen made for him.

The Chilterns are a low chalk range lying across Buckinghamshire and on into parts of Oxfordshire and Hertfordshire. Dense beech forests sheltered many an outlaw from Saxon times onwards, until it became necessary to create the office of Steward of the Chiltern Hundreds with authority to hunt them down and keep the place clear. It was this woodland which also provided the material for High Wycombe's furniture industry, and which still gives employment to a few remaining practitioners of the old craft of chairbodging. The bodger works day in, day out, all year round, in a primitive shelter in the woods. As trees are thinned out, he gets busy on the spot, cutting out chair legs from freshly felled timber and thereby saving the labour and expense of carting whole trunks—including the proportion which will inevitably go to waste—to the factory. Discarded strips and fragments can often be used for making tent pegs.

From Hambleden it is no great distance to Fingest, a Saxon settlement with a descriptive name, *pinghyrst* identifying 'the wooded mound of the assembly'. The church has a thick-walled Norman tower on which, four centuries later, a double-gabled saddleback roof was set. The village was for years the home of a well-known figure of our own time, 'Cassandra' of the *Daily Mirror*.

A mile away is the pretty village of Turville, close to luxuriant woodlands in the Wormsley valley, and dominated by a lofty, weather-boarded smock mill, sail-less not so many years ago but now splendidly restored. In the near vicinity are traces of small Norman encampments: the ditch around the vicarage garden may be one such. They were established when Saxons refusing to accept the writ of the Norman invaders hid away in the beech forests and launched sporadic raids on the countryside and on any Norman travellers rash enough not to travel in sufficiently powerful numbers. The church of St Mary is basically Norman, and has a fine heraldic window. At the turn of the century, restoration work revealed a large stone coffin under the floor, containing two skeletons. One of them was that of a woman with a suspicious hole in her skull. Amateur detectives tried to trace her identity through parish records, and no doubt there was some speculation in the village about foul play in old local families; but no writer of fact or fiction has, so far as I know, ever come up with any explanation of the death and the double burial.

While in the Chilterns we ought to be prodded by the names of Great Hampden and Little Hampden into paying our respects to that village where the squire John Hampden made his great declaration. In the church of Great Kimble, under the western slope of the hills, a meeting was held in 1637 at which Hampden denounced Charles I's exactions of 'ship money' and other unconstitutional levies, and refused to pay. From such demands and such defiance stemmed, inexorably, the Civil War.

On the heights—six hundred feet up, in fact—is Nettlebed, which the eighteenth-century German traveller Karl Philip Moritz considered the perfect village. He noted that the farmers, unlike those of his native land, were dressed 'in good cloth and good taste'. The vocal and instrumental music in church on Sunday delighted him, with only the haughtiness of the preacher to add a discordant note. Each time he tried to continue his journey he felt reluctant to leave, and very nearly decided to stay an extra week. When he summoned up the courage to go, he kept looking back at the church tower and the clustering cottages where he had been so much at home; and did so with a heavy heart. Today it is the surrounding countryside which charms, rather than the village itself. For centuries it has been associated with brick making, and still has a brick kiln behind its main street.

The gravestone to a village blacksmith, William Strange, reads:

> *My Sledge and Anvil lie declined,*
> *My bellows too have lost their Wind;*
> *My Fire's extinct, my Forge decayed,*
> *And in the Dust my Vice is laid;*
> *My Coals are spent, my Iron's gone,*
> *My Nails are drove; my Work is done.*

A blacksmith of the next century, Benjamin Linton of Blean in Kent, is commemorated in almost the same words, but in the third person instead of the first.

Water supplies to these hilltop settlements were often problematical. Stoke Row received unexpected help in this direction in 1864. A local engineer, Edward Anderson Reade of Ipsden House,

had been working for the Maharajah of Benares and casually told him of the difficulties back home. As a personal gift the Maharajah paid for the sinking of a 350-foot well, capped by an oriental dome on pillars which, approached through an avenue of yews, gives the appearance of a little shrine.

Lower-lying Ewelme has no lack of water. Its very name means 'source of a river', and since the seventeenth century there have been extensive watercress beds along the stream through the village from the King's Pool. The king in question here was Henry VIII, who is reputed to have been skittishly pushed into the pond by a lady-in-waiting. This may have taken place during Henry's honeymoon with Catherine of Aragon, which was spent at a palace which has now become the local manor house. In the church is buried Alice, Duchess of Suffolk and granddaughter of Geoffrey Chaucer, her tomb showing her in two guises: one with full court dress, the other in a shroud. Her almshouses are still occupied, but the residents do not have to wear the once-prescribed cloaks bearing a red cross. The village school, from the same date, is thought to be the oldest still in use in the country.

Buried in the churchyard is Jerome K. Jerome, author of *Three Men in a Boat*.

Which takes us happily enough back to the Thames.

Near the Goring gap which the river cuts through the hills, Pangbourne and Whitchurch join hands across the water by means of a toll bridge. Here the bourne of the Pang enters the Thames, and here any number of stray threads of water curl through Whitchurch, so that at times the pedestrian might think himself in some Broadland village such as Horning: there are little moorings instead of car ports, as many boathouses as garages, waterside gardens and waterside paths; and just when the paths seem in danger of running out there are footbridges. Hardly surprising that the local pub is the *Ferryboat* or that among its windows it has a number of brass-rimmed portholes.

On into Oxfordshire, and we reach a spot as well loved by Oxford undergraduates as Grantchester is by those of Cambridge. I, too, shared the pleasures of the *Trout* inn beside the bridge and lock when, during the Second World War, I was stationed not too far from Godstow. Its most imposing neighbour is Blenheim Palace, on the edge of whose park Sir Winston Churchill and his father, Lord Randolph Churchill, are buried in Bladon village churchyard. Within that park once stood Woodstock Manor, birthplace of the Black Prince; and before that, a maze at the heart of which Henry II kept his beloved mistress Rosamund, 'a rare and peerless piece' according to Holinshed. Rosamund Clifford came originally from Frampton-on-Severn in Gloucestershire, where one of the largest village greens in the country is still called Rosamund's Green. An old story tells how Henry's jealous wife, Eleanor of Aquitaine, found her way through the maze with the aid of a silken thread, and offered Fair Rosamund the choice of death by dagger or poison. Rosamund chose poison. But more sober chronicles say she died a natural death in 1176 and was buried in the nunnery at Godstow. Her tombstone was somewhat reproving:

> The rose of the world, but not the clean flower,
>   Is now here graven, to whom beauty was lent.
> In this grave, full dark, is now her bower,
>   That by her life was sweet and redolent.
> But now that she is from this life blent,
>   Though she were sweet, now foully doth she stink,
> A mirror, good, for all men that on her think.

How can anyone have the temerity to nominate a small selection of villages as being truly representative of the Midland Shires? From the spires and fox-hunting squires of Northamptonshire through Rutland and Leicestershire to the Shakespeare country of Warwickshire and the orchards of Worcestershire ... there are too many contrasts for any one place, or even a score of places, to be declared typical. If one hamlet, one church, one bridge stays in the memory it may be because of some personal reaction, some sympathetic resonance which will last a lifetime without any friend, no matter how close, ever catching even the whisper of its echo.

The chequered timber and plaster of Worcestershire and Warwickshire, or its red or lime-washed brick nogging, may have a more immediate visual appeal than the stone of Northamptonshire or the rust-brown villages of Rutland; but look again, and again—and wait for the subtler magic to work.

There are three major quarries in the east of the region whose stones have coloured towns and villages far towards the west. Clipsham's coarse, hard limestone comes in light buff shades like vanilla fudge, and can be seen in Canterbury, Ripon and Peterborough cathedrals, and in Buckingham Palace and the House of Commons. Colly Weston has been producing autumn-brown limestone slates since Roman times, thin but hard-wearing, generally used at a steep pitch. The slopes of Colly Weston village itself display the local product on precipitous little roofs and perky slate-capped dormers, looking out over the far shimmering plain and the rising slopes of Rutland.

Another buff-coloured stone comes from Weldon quarry, its weathering qualities finding a sturdy advertisement in the Eleanor Crosses at Hardingstone and Geddington. The original sequence of these monuments marked stopping places on the funeral journey to London of Eleanor of Castile, wife to Edward I, after her death at Harby, Lincolnshire, in 1290. The third surviving cross is at Waltham Cross in Hertfordshire; and there is of course a replica at Charing Cross, the corpse's last halt before its ultimate resting place at Westminster. The Geddington cross is sculpted like a tall, slender font cover, standing on a stepped plinth above an old well. It makes a fitting companion to the fourteenth-century tower and spire of the church.

To the west, on a ridge from which spring the Avon, the Welland and the Nene, is Naseby. A stone column just over a mile north of the village marks the battlefield where the New Model Army under Fairfax and Cromwell in 1645 met the Royalists under Prince Rupert and King Charles himself, forcing Charles to flee for his life and resulting in the capture of incriminating documents which showed once and for all the insincerity of all his earlier pretences at negotiation. The presumed site of Cromwell's crucial cavalry charge is also marked, south of Naseby.

Shifts of county boundaries must have perplexed many villagers at one time and another. Thanks to the varying allegiances of the

Soke of Peterborough, certain communities have found themselves one year in Northamptonshire, another in Huntingdonshire. And poor little Rutland, having fought several battles to preserve its independence, was at last swallowed up in 1974.

Wansford on the Nene dodges the issue by declaring itself Wansford-in-England. This is said to result from the activities of a seventeenth-century drunkard who, reeling home to find the dreaded plague sign on his own door, stumbled off to spend the night in a haycock. While he snored the river flooded and carried him away, and he awoke without a notion of what was going on. When people from the banks laughed and called to ask where he was from, he replied that he came from Wansford Brigs in England.

The bridge is a noble span of ten arches, a survival of the Middle Ages threatened by traffic on the Great North Road until that was mercifully diverted and refashioned as the A1.

Helpston now belongs officially to Huntingdonshire, though I should never be surprised to hear that it has been nudged back where it belongs. Its most famous son, commemorated by a rather Disney-ish monument topped by a cross, and by a plaque on his cottage, certainly regarded himself and has been thought of ever since as a Northamptonshire poet. And it was in Northampton, in a mental asylum, that John Clare ended his days. He was mad; but saw truths and remembered beauties with a vividness rarely matched by the so-called sane. His village is still secluded, in a rural maze of unhurried lanes through rich oak woods. And his thatched cottage is as he always saw it, reaching out through the haze of despair and bewilderment:

> *The old house stooped just like a cave,*
> *Thatched o'er with mosses green,*
> *Winter around the walls did rave,*
> *But all was calm within,*
> *The trees are here all green agen,*
> *Here bees the flowers still kiss,*
> *But flowers and trees seemed sweeter then,*
> *My early home was this.*

Rutland—for we shall continue to think of it as Rutland, a separate entity, for a long time yet—is at first sight a surprisingly deserted county. Its entire population is one-tenth that of the city of Leicester, its new master. Out of its gentle undulations jut sudden ridges and hillocks, and on these most of the villages have been perched. Many would almost seem to have been jammed on the crown of their hill around the church and then begun to slip, so that from each tower or spire there is a brownstone cascade down the slope, with splashes of grey brick and large smudges of Colly Weston slate. Whitwell, Empingham, the Hambletons, Burley . . . such a smoothly switchback countryside. And there's Edith Weston, named after the wife of Edward the Confessor who was granted this corner of Rutland.

Perhaps the villages are stacked up there out of the way in order to get a better view of, or keep out of the path of, the huntsmen whose favourite domain this is. Two famous hunts share Rutland: one, created by the Duke of Rutland, became the Belvoir; the other was the Earl of Gainsborough's and began its long career at Exton in 1732, moving its kennels to Cottesmore some fifty years later. Now their home is at Ashwell, a one-time green village whose green has been removed, but the name of the pack remains the Cottesmore. The village of Cottesmore itself is a rich golden-brown blend of cottages and church, topped by the pinnacle of a thirteenth-century broach spire.

The red coats are much in force in Leicestershire, too; but it is with two very different men that we associate two quiet little villages in the county. In 1725 Robert Bakewell was born in a farmhouse at Dishley, and applied himself from an early age to rearing sheep. He travelled widely to study comparative methods and to find new stock, and it has been said that he virtually invented several new breeds. On his own model farm, irrigated by a mile-long canal, he experimented with the fattening of sheep and cattle to provide more food for the growing populations in new industrial towns. He put his best rams and bulls out to stud, and acquired such a reputation that he could soon charge what fees he chose. It was said by envious critics that 'his animals were too dear for any one to buy and too fat for any one to eat'. The walls of his home were hung with animal skeletons and with choice anatomical specimens pickled in brine so that he could explain breeding points to distinguished visitors from all over the world. As we have seen, Coke of Norfolk was not too proud to call him in for advice, and Bakewell spent a constructive week at Holkham. But he always came back to Dishley, and died here in 1795.

The following century produced another innovator. Hathern still has its old village cross and its old, rather heavily restored, fourteenth-century church. It also has the timbered and thatched cottages in one of which John Heathcoat was born. In 1808 this young man solved the problem of producing machine-made net for pillow lace which would not unravel, by devising a bobbin net machine whose twisting motion has remained an essential feature of modern counterparts. When he married he decided to go into business a couple of miles away in Loughborough. The outcome was, in the climate of those times, predictable. Alarmed by the efficiency of Heathcoat's machines, the Luddites smashed them and showed every sign of finishing off the inventor too. He and his wife moved far away to Tiverton in Devon, and in 1816 established a net-making industry which did much to revive the town after its decline as a wool centre.

Twycross is a name which sets up a purely personal love–hate twinge in me. In 1941 I spent some months there learning—or failing to learn—some of the mysteries of radar: spent them, that is, at nearby Gopsall Hall, which I seemed to recall was about two miles from the gate of its vast park, and embedded in a sea of wintry mud. We were frequently held up in our studies by the absence of an essential power cable, which usually proved to have been borrowed by a young subaltern who wanted to play the organ in the great house. The benign phantom of a once frequent guest would doubtless have approved: Handel stayed here often with his friend Charles Jennens, and is thought to have composed part of *Messiah* on the premises. Our jaundiced view was that he did so because there was absolutely nothing else to do in such a bleak spot. Nevertheless I felt a mild pang of regret when I heard that, although

Wyattville's flamboyant entrance arch still stands, the hall was pulled down in 1951.

In Twycross village the church has some remarkable glass. It is about seven hundred years old, but arrived here only in the time of William IV. When there were fears that the beautiful Sainte Chapelle in Paris might be desecrated during the French Revolution, the most precious glass was removed and later sold to an Englishman. In due course it was presented to the King, who in turn gave some of it to Earl Howe, who gave it to Twycross. Originally it was believed that all the glass came from the one source, but later investigation shows that some of it, including the Presentation in the Temple, probably belonged to other Parisian churches.

The Midland Plain stretches west to the Welsh heights, and northwards under the ridges of the Peak and the Pennines. Although we think instinctively of it in terms of the Black Country, the Potteries, the factories and the conurbations of Wolverhampton, Birmingham and Coventry, the region in fact kept its woodlands longer than did the now rural Weald. Clearings were intermittent, unco-ordinated; so that now, with the forest cloak largely stripped away, we can trace no discernible pattern in the placing or growth of settlements. Also, there are few true green villages: when makeshift paths between scattered hamlets solidified into regular roads, such villages as flourished did so by reaching out along the roads.

Many villages did not flourish. A number of sites had been abandoned well before the beginning of the seventeenth century. They can be traced by intersections of trodden-over pathways, occasional mounds, and the outlines of cottages or farm buildings. In Warwickshire alone, over a hundred have been identified. In Shropshire, villages which were once developed to form part of the defence works along the Welsh border dwindled with the fading of military necessity, so that many settlements today are little more than hamlets, often without church or pub.

The magic names of Sherwood Forest and the Forest of Arden account, in their way, for the commonest building styles across the Midlands. Limestone is used, from the soft oolite of the Cotswolds to the harder rock of the north-east; but with such a wealth of timber to hand, it is hardly surprising that this should be the country of timber—of sturdy frame construction and of ambitious patterns in blackened wood and white plaster. Even when brick was more frequently used as a replacement for mud and plaster, it was whitewashed to give a similar effect.

These are the houses we associate with 'Shakespeare country': houses almost invariably festooned with climbing plants or hollyhocks and others which give the impression that the timbers have suddenly come to life again and started putting out exotic shoots. At Wilmcote is the fine Tudor yeoman's house where Mary Arden was born. The stone dovecot, a veritable apartment block, has been preserved, and some of the original farm buildings house a small museum of local crafts and relics. From here Mary Arden went to wed John Shakespeare at Aston Cantlow, and in due time to produce a son William.

Just outside Stratford-upon-Avon, the plentifully thatched village of Shottery stands up with difficulty to the unrelenting influx of tourists bent on seeing the cottage where young Will courted Anne Hathaway. It is no use quibbling that the title of their goal is a misnomer: it was not Anne Hathaway's cottage, but that of her step-mother, with whom Anne went on living after her father's death, and it is not a cottage but a deep-thatched house of a dozen rooms; but it will now never be known as anything else, and millions will believe that in one of those rooms, on a holy relic of a bench, the Bard wooed the rather plain Anne, eight years older than himself. Anne had been pregnant for some months before they married, and it has even been suggested that Will wanted to marry someone else but was forced into this liaison by the determined young woman. However that may be, there are plenty of lanes and plenty of riverside walks round here which the romantically inclined may believe to have known their footsteps.

Passing by Wilmcote on its way from Stratford to Kingswood is a 13½-mile section of the Stratford Canal reopened in 1964 by the Queen Mother. The original canal, which cost half a million pounds to construct, had been abandoned for thirty years but now, under the benevolent management of the National Trust, provides a delightful route for pleasure craft. One of the most striking features of the original concept was the long descent to Stratford by a system of thirty-six locks.

The canals, so many of them now abandoned or at best rescued piecemeal for recreational purposes, played a formative role in the story of town and village development and decay. 'Canal mania', like the railway craze so soon after, dictated whether your community became a viable commercial proposition or, in every sense of the word, a backwater. Coal and iron could be more easily and economically transported by water than along the rutted and often swampy roads. Junctions of waterways became as important as crossroads; as important as, and similar to, the later railway junctions where goods could be transhipped or shunted on to another line, parked in a dock or siding, stored in warehouses for collection. And there were not merely freight-carrying barges: villagers and farmers along the route could more easily and comfortably get into the local market town for business and shopping, and the regular packet services did a brisk trade. Terraced red-brick villages grew up near the basins and the sheds. Men were needed to load and unload barges, and to operate the horse tramroads—1500 miles of them during the boom era—feeding stone and coal to the network. On the Trent and Mersey canal, Froghall owed its very existence to the traffic in limestone from Caldon Low quarries.

Other hastily constructed settlements grew from the improvised homes of workers supplied by the canal operators with raw materials. The chain-makers and nailers of Cradley Heath and Blackheath were squatters, as the smallholders of the forests had once been squatters; then their communities grew into villages, just as the settlements of the woodland clearings had grown; but if these industrial settlements prospered, they ceased to be villages and were drawn into an unplanned huddle which became willy-nilly a town.

Dudley is in Worcestershire, and so is Halesowen; but so, too, are the villages under the Malverns and the blossom-drowned villages of the Vale of Evesham. And so is Broadway, the 'painted lady of the Cotswolds'. Perhaps that phrase deserves a few more capitals: one would like to think of Broadway as a glowing butterfly rather than a country girl of ill repute. It has become dangerously large, bidding fair to lose its village status and turn into a small town. It needs only another street of antique shops, a tourist hotel, perhaps a factory for *making* enough antiques to keep up with the demand ... But one feels it will manage to keep disaster at bay. The shops are, at present, genuine enough. No new hotel would offer serious competition to the seventeenth-century *Lygon Arms*, and it would be impossible to emulate the little *Fish* inn. As to factories, there is one already, firmly settled into the community. The Gordon Russell family started in 1924 to repair the valuable old furniture of the *Lygon Arms*, and now have a reputation not only for skilled restoration work but for the quality of their own products. Their showrooms are open to the public on certain days.

On the site of a gibbet where three innocent people were hanged in the seventeenth century for a crime they didn't commit is a cross-hands signpost. And on the hill above the village is a beacon tower built in 1797. But it is not the detail that counts; not the isolated historic curiosity. One should see Broadway whole, descending the hill at a leisurely pace (if impatient following traffic will allow) and taking in the consistent yet unrepetitive avenue of Cotswold stone down both sides of the wide street. It was made by craftsmen who cared for the material they used, and knew how best to present it, and all the clicking of cameras and the gazing of trippers will not erode it. After all, unless we are lucky enough to live in such a place, are we not all trippers and gazers?

The colour of the stone grows harsher if we head north into Shropshire. Red sandstone appears in the base of many timber-framed houses, supporting many a fine pattern in wood and plaster, or wood and colour-washed brick. But the overall effect can be dulled by a preponderance of Welsh slate, which acquires no velvety moss, no slightly furred patina, but remains simply what it is—grey slate.

From Grinshill quarries, north of Shrewsbury, came two distinctive types of building stone, referred to as red and white, though in fact the gradations run from brown through an odd sort of luminescent pink to pale grey-green.

Tong is one of the county's most attractive villages: Dickens found it so, and said he visualized it as the setting for the last part of *The Old Curiosity Shop*. Here the red sandstone is very much in evidence in St Bartholomew's church, with its finely battlemented tower. It has been called a Westminster Abbey in miniature because of its imposing congregation of alabaster monuments, and the sixteenth-century Golden Chapel has some impressive fan vaulting.

A few miles to the east are the church ruins of the twelfth-century White Ladies Priory. Fleeing from his victorious enemies after the battle of Worcester, Charles II made his way here to hide in the house of the loyal Penderells, and then went on to Boscobel House. As the search for him intensified, it was considered too risky for him to stay indoors during the day, so he climbed up into the bushy branches of a large oak in the grounds and remained there until nightfall. During the hours of darkness he made his way on again and joined Lord Wilmot, to continue his journey towards Bristol disguised as a serving man. After the Restoration the tree was cut to pieces by souvenir hunters, but the present 'Royal Oak' is said to have been grown from an acorn of the original tree on the original site.

Clun museum displays a well arranged selection of historical finds which depict and clarify the whole settlement pattern of the area from prehistoric times to the present day.

As an almost self-explanatory picture of the growth and decline of a settlement, it would be hard to beat Moreton Corbet. The Norman mother church of St Mary's at Shawbury founded a number of chapels in the locality, one of them at Moreton Corbet. It is clear that the village was in reasonable shape at that period, and continued to be so until the early sixteenth century. Its general shape and the shape of the medieval earthworks are still discernible, dominated by a small Norman keep and the remains of a gatehouse. Then alterations were made to what was left of the original castle, and a new manor in the classical style was begun for Robert Corbet in 1579. It would obviously have been very fine if it had ever been finished. During construction, a large park was developed, the road was diverted, and the villagers moved out. There is no record of their having been rehoused in a fresh settlement, and Corbet died before his own house could be completed. During the Civil War the Royalists put a garrison into the castle, which, together with most of the manor house, was burnt by the Parliamentarians.

CHAPTER SEVEN

The Backbone

From Kinder Scout, 'The Peak' of the Peak District, the footpath of the Pennine Way stretches two hundred and fifty miles to the Cheviots. The moors and mountains it crosses are infinitely wilder and more awe-inspiring than the pastures of the North or South Downs Way; but the villages, remote and grey as some of them may seem, are just as hospitable. Grey stone and grey slate can be forbidding at first glance. No romantic thatch and precious little timber here. But with familiarity grows affection, and in many places outright admiration for the homogeneity of the materials and the building styles. Set below the 'edges' of hill and ridge, stepped up in trim terraces and toiling sturdily up eccentrically angled slopes, the villages make up in harmony what they lack in individual dazzle. Their fabric is, after all, only a human rearrangement of the rough mountain limestone and gritstone on which they stand. And out in the fields, instead of hedges there are the incredible miles of drystone walls, still in perfect keeping with the farms they enclose and with the stark moors whose long-forgotten monastic sheep-runs they still define. A labour which would have caused even Hercules to throw up his hands in despair would be that of counting the number of stones in any square mile of those walls.

Crich, in eastern Derbyshire where the hills begin to climb towards the Peak District National Park, is an attractive example. Set high, with splendid views all round, it looks like—and is—an industrial village; but a clean, gleaming monochrome one. How is it that the streets are so free from litter? As for the industry, it's a very ancient one. Lead ore was dug out of the Pennines and out of the Peak before the Romans came, and the Romans continued the extraction: from time to time their pigs or ingots are found, and can be localized by the identifying letters inscribed in them. Saxons and Danes mined here—the Odin Mine near Castleton takes its name from supposed

Scandinavian connections—and Domesday Book lists a number of lead works, one of them at Crich.

In more recent centuries, the lead has been only a by-product of mining for limestone, for roadworks and for lime burning. Some vast geological upheaval thrust up a limestone mass at Crich, known as Crich crag—'crag' itself being the Saxon word from which Crich is derived. When George Stephenson was working on the North Midland railway he opened up Cliff Quarry here to provide limestone for the Ambergate kilns. A tramway was installed, operated by horses and inclined cable haulage. Then came steam, and later diesel. The quarry was closed in 1957, but has since been reopened for a new purpose. A tramway museum preserves here a collection of town tramcars from all over Britain, with a few foreign examples. Track has been laid along the bed of the quarry so that visitors can ride in Glasgow or Sheffield cars, inside or on open balconies upstairs. There are single-deckers and double-deckers, a horse-drawn tram from Portugal, and a fine old specimen from Prague, repaired and painted up for delivery to Crich in 1968 just two days before the Russians entered Czechoslovakia.

Throughout the region, and throughout the summer, an old custom not merely survives but seems to gain competitive strength each year. Where water is, in spite of heavy rainfall, so short on the limestone heights, fertility rituals must have been practised since pagan times. Taken over by Christianity, they blossomed out into the richly imaginative custom of well-dressing. By a village spring or tap, decorative panels of leaves and flower petals, moss and pebbles will be constructed on a background of wet clay. The subjects are usually Biblical, and it has become a matter of parochial pride to create the largest and most elaborate picture. Most contestants will reluctantly concede, though, that Tissington, with its five wells, usually comes top of the league table.

Tissington is at any time of the year a bright and welcoming little place: in every sense a model village, still under the benevolent eye of the Fitzherberts in their Jacobean manor. There are some good family monuments in the church, one angelically aspiring into the roof, and also a remarkably carved Norman doorway and font, and a two-decker pulpit.

So that competing villagers have a chance of attending their rivals' displays and services, the ceremonies of blessing the wells are staggered throughout the season. Tissington traditionally celebrates its well-dressing on Ascension Day, Hope may combine it with Wakes Week, Eyam saves it for August.

Eyam has another, less happy annual commemoration. In September 1665 a tailor living in Cooper's Cottage by the church had a consignment of cloth sent to him from London. As the material was damp he hung it up in front of the fire. A few days later, complaining of the sweet, sickly smell in his nostrils, he died. The sons of the widow with whom he shared the cottage were the next to go, and then a couple from the neighbouring cottage. The plague had reached the village.

Two men whose views were bitterly opposed and who might well have been enemies decided to join forces. They were William Mompesson, the Anglican rector, and Thomas Stanley, the Puritan who had been dismissed for refusing to implement the Act of Uniformity. They preached a joint sermon, imploring the villagers not to give way to panic and desert the village. Instead, they should seal themselves off from the world until the plague was over, rather than spread it across the countryside. Few inhabitants defected. One who did so was stoned by neighbouring villagers to keep her at her distance. The Earl of Devonshire arranged for food to be sent to the brave garrison, paid for by money left in a mixture of water and vinegar at what is now called Mompesson's Well. Rather than crowd people together in the church, the rector carried on services in the open air from a rock which came to be known as Cucklet Church.

The reward of courage was the death of two hundred and fifty people. Ninety survived. Among the survivors were Mompesson's two children, whom, in spite of his stern injunctions to others, he smuggled out to safety one night. His wife died, and is buried in the churchyard. She was one of very few to be so: most corpses were hurried out to improvised graves in the fields, or dug into the village ground where they lay. A family called the Talbots are to be found in what is now a pleasant orchard; the Hancocks—father, three sons and three daughters—were carried out to a bleak hillside and buried there, one by one, by the man's widow. On the Sunday after the well-dressing, village women put on seventeenth-century costume and take part in a Plague Sunday service in the dell of Cucklet Church.

Behind the village the road climbs to fine hillside levels which never stay level for long, but offer exhilarating vistas of further hills, as if to blow away the sadness of the community's affliction. And as we go on into the High Peak—a name which is rather confusing, since the word 'Peak' refers not to summits but to the old Celtic tribe of the Peacs—we see what often appear to be small cairns, burial mounds, or small drystone shelters. Most of them, here and on through the Pennines and over the moors, mark old pit-heads; and what might be crumbling chapels are the remains of old engine-houses.

This is walking country, for those with stout boots and stout lungs. Hayfield, today a popular departure point for the way up Kinder Scout, can reasonably claim to be the place where the doors were opened to The Peak and to hundreds of miles beyond. Until after the Second World War, access to the most enticing of these uplands was severely restricted by landowners anxious to preserve them exclusively for rearing and shooting their game. In 1932 a mass demonstration at Hayfield called for a 'mass trespass' on Kinder Scout, and had to be broken up by police and gamekeepers. Some spokesmen for the campaign were sent to prison, but the demand continued for the creation of a Pennine Way 'as a natural heritage of the youth of the country and of all who feel the call of the hills and the lonely places'. This was answered in 1949 by the National Parks and Access to the Countryside Act, incorporating plans for the extension of tracks and bridlepaths. The English, according to Moritz in 1782, are on the whole 'too rich or too lazy' to walk. One wonders how he would have reacted to the gathering of over two thousand people on Malham Moor in April 1965 to celebrate the completion of the Pennine Way; or to the thousands of young people

who set out every year with rucksacks and high hopes along those
apparently forbidding ridgeways.

To give him his due, Karl Philip Moritz was a bit of a pioneer.
At a time when the average Englishman viewed a hiker (though the
term had not yet been invented) as the most contemptible sort of
peasant, to be treated with disdain in wayside hostelries and with a
suspicion equal to that of the modern Los Angeles automobile driver
towards a pedestrian, this German chose to tramp the country in
order to see what it really looked and felt like. On one occasion,
though, he accepted a lift in unusual circumstances. Anxious to in-
spect the Peak Cavern at Castleton, he was carried across the stream
known as the Styx on the back of a guide whose voice and aspect
were 'so fitting to the character of Charon' that the name of the
rivulet occasioned no surprise. Entering the great arch of the cave
they went down the sloping path into twilight:

> And when we had gone forward a few steps, what a sight I saw!
> Looking to my right I glimpsed a complete village below the vast
> wall of the cavern. As it was Sunday the villagers had a day off
> work and were sitting before their huts with their children. We
> had hardly left these tiny dwellings behind when we came to a
> number of large wheels, used by the subterranean villagers for
> rope-making. It was as if I were gazing upon the wheel of Ixion
> and the unending toil of the Danaides.

Today the entrance to the cavern remains blackened by the smoke
from the chimneys and fireplaces of those troglodyte settlers, and
the footings of their homes are still visible. Modern visitors, arriving
in parties of twenty or thirty and more, can hardly expect to be
carried around as Moritz was on the shoulders of their guide. Exploring the caves is almost as arduous a holiday occupation as striding
out across the moors. There are boats to negotiate the water-plopping
tunnels of the Speedwell Cavern; flights of steps up and down
through the grottoes of Treak Cliff with its streaks of Blue John
fluorspar and its stalactite valances; and sometimes ragged, sometimes slippery rock underfoot and arching overhead in the Peak
Cavern, which Walter Scott called the Devil's Cavern. Clinging to

the hillside above this last is the fortress of Peveril of the Peak, of which Scott made good use in one of his novels. Attainable from one direction only, it remained well-nigh impregnable for centuries. Now a zig-zag path up the steep slope joins it to a side street out of the grey, compact little village—a shapely little place to be avoided over Bank Holiday weekends.

Castleton, too, has an annual ceremony all its own. On Oak Apple Day, 29 May, known here as Garland Day, there is a carnival procession loosely related to the Restoration of Charles II in 1660. A king wearing a beribboned, bell-shaped cage decorated with flowers makes a circuit of the village accompanied by his carnival queen and children dressed in white, and there is revelry round a maypole set up in the market-place. At the end of the rejoicing the garland is roped up to the church tower and left there to wither.

On the Staffordshire rim of the Peak District is what claims to be the highest village in England, with the highest parish church. This is Flash, where one cottage maintains a meteorological service every other hour to Manchester airport. It has a reputation for other activities, less savoury. At one time it was the Mecca of the prize-fighting and cock-fighting fraternities, and still has traces of two cock-pits. Being so close to the junction of three county boundaries—Staffordshire, Cheshire and Derbyshire—it offered a variety of escape routes if the local authority chose to pounce. It also gave its name to 'flash' coins, having gone in for counterfeiting pewter currency; while on the respectable side it carried on a small local industry in cloth-covered buttons.

Not far away is Longnor, on the side of a ridge beyond which a plunging, soaring and twisting road leads to Dovedale. It has gritty back lanes and cobbled setts, and seems to belong somewhere else and to another time; but I have never quite decided where or when. One would not be surprised to find that, as at Chatsworth, gates could bar all roads into or out of a village which on one side of its little square has the *Crewe and Harpur Arms*, and on the other a table of tolls payable by sellers and buyers at the market, laid down by order of Sir Vauncy Harpur Crewe, Lord of the Manor of Longnor, in 1903.

And there's Alstonfield, which has two adjoining greens in the heart of the village, each with its own chestnut tree. One suspects that the greens were originally one, before somebody cut a slice of road through them. There is a craft centre; and a sign offers 'Teas at the Post Office', with no indication as to whether there are first-class and second-class teas, with a longer wait for the latter.

Daniel Defoe, when visiting the Peak during the first quarter of the eighteenth century, had a look at the little spa of Quarndon but found it inferior to Tunbridge Wells or Epsom and decided to press on:

> From Quarndon we advanced due north, and, mounting the hills gradually for four or five miles, we soon had a most frightful view indeed among the black mountains of the Peak; however, as they were yet at a distance, and a good town lay on our left called Wirksworth, we turned thither for refreshment. Here indeed we found a specimen of what I had heard before, viz. that however rugged the hills were, the vales were everywhere fruitful, well inhabited, the markets well supplied, and the provisions extraordinarily good; not forgetting the ale, which everywhere exceeded, if possible, what was passed, as if the farther north the better the liquor, and that the nearer we approached to Yorkshire, as the place for the best, so the ale advanced the nearer to its perfection.

Standards of the vales and dales, the markets and provisions cannot be faulted this two hundred and fifty years later. I cannot say the same about the ale. But let us nevertheless follow Defoe's optimistic plunge into Yorkshire.

For much of the way we are in fact treading a Pennine tightrope between Yorkshire and Lancashire, Northumbria and Cumbria, wondering which way to jump. The smoke of industrial towns gouged into the rock deters us; the fertile valleys invite. Ahead, heathery moorland the colour of dried blood, and stones darkened by age rather than by fumes. The drystone walls go on and on, and then crumble where both field and farmstead have been abandoned. There are craggy teeth along the walls of roofless cottages and around the mine-workings. Not much older in appearance are other ruined enclosures and cairns which prove to be the remains of Bronze Age villages.

High Withens on Haworth Moor might conceivably be the steading of some warrior farmer from an Icelandic saga. To Emily Brontë it was *Wuthering Heights*.

Haworth Parsonage is set back from the top of the steep village street whose setts are, in places, as treacherous in wet weather as they must have been to horses in the Brontës' time. From one side of the house, windows look out over the graveyard; from another, over the moor which provided background and inspiration for much of their writing. Patrick Brontë took up the incumbency in 1820, bringing with him his wife and six children: two daughters had been born at Hartshead, and three more daughters and a son at the parsonage in Thornton. Anne, the youngest, was only a few months old when they reached Haworth—'a moorland parish where', according to Charlotte, there was not 'a single educated family'. They had not been installed long when Mrs Brontë died; and within a few years the two eldest daughters followed her. The other girls, with few playmates, created their own world of poetic fantasy, to which their brother Branwell contributed when he was not drinking himself into a state of sullen despair. Branwell died of consumption in September 1848; Charlotte, who had caught a chill at his funeral, tried to carry on her domestic duties in the damp, cold parsonage, and herself died in December. Anne was to follow by the next May.

The house today does not seem cold or gloomy. Its position gives it sunlight from one side or another during most of the day—but the sun does not shine all year round in these parts, and the winters must have been terrible for the always delicate girls. The rooms of the parsonage have been arranged, according to Mrs Gaskell's descriptions, as closely as possible to their condition when the Brontës occupied them. An extra wing has been added to expand the museum. It is nearly always crowded. As a place of literary pilgrimage it can surely have no serious rival. Inevitably the teetering, tottering street outside, though little changed architecturally, has adapted its shop windows to suit the market. There is hardly one which does not advertise some kind of Brontë tourist-ware, and it comes as quite a shock to find there is no huge board outside the smartened-up *Black Bull* inn by the churchyard, declaring that Branwell drank himself to death on the premises.

Once the girls could walk across a field or two when shopping in Keighley. Now town and village have well-nigh coalesced. Still it is not difficult to get away from the mills and chimneys. In a few minutes, as audiences for the film of E. Nesbit's *The Railway Children* will know, the train has carried one into a sylvan landscape. Where once the smoke and steam of its engine might have been regarded as an additional cause of pollution, today it is cherished just as the out-moded trams of Crich are cherished. The Worth Valley Railway, saved from extinction by a band of enthusiasts, has collected since 1965 a specimen of almost every type of steam locomotive that ever operated in Britain, from little shunters up to a Pacific class engine which once used to pull the Golden Arrow. They are kept partly in the goods yard and sheds at Haworth, partly on covered sidings at Oxenhope, at the far end of the line from Keighley.

North-east of Keighley and beyond one of the most celebrated moors, Ilkley Moor, lies a village with an unappetizing name: Blub-berhouses. It is in fact one of the most attractive little hamlets in the region. The villages of Wharfedale and those tucked away on the tangled roads towards Pateley Bridge are all well aware of their good fortune. There are few more satisfying drives than that from Bolton Abbey, on its lovely curve of river, along the winding dale to Gras-sington. Where the road comes down to meadow level is Burnsall bridge, spanning the Wharfe beside the inn and little cluster of com-fortably weathered houses. Although the population is less than a hundred, it once supported a famous grammar school, now converted to a primary school. Furthermore, two parsons once officiated here, each with his own parsonage and a separate pulpit and reading desk in the church. The parish was divided in 1876. On the annual sports day there is a fell race, up a course climbing a thousand feet on the fell. The record time for the overall run of a mile is 12 minutes 59.8 seconds, unchallenged since 1910.

From Grassington, which is either the most prosperous village or the smartest and best conceived little town in northern England, the road swoops and climbs eastwards over moorland littered with old mining relics, cottages falling to bits and, appropriately enough, a grey pub called the *Miner's Arms* hunched against the prevailing wind. At Pateley Bridge there tends to be a gathering of caravans, but within a few minutes we can be on a narrow, unclassified road winding its way along the bank of delectable Gouthwaite reservoir. A packhorse bridge, thought to have been built six hundred years ago by the monks of Fountains Abbey, leads into Wath; or, if you choose to continue along the reservoir, leads out of Wath towards its hemp mill. The water-wheel, which continued working until 1967, is the second largest in Britain, and makes an impressive sight thrusting out from the wall of what is now the *Watermill Inn*. The owners of this hotel and restaurant helpfully allow access to the mill itself at all reasonable times.

It is no use being in a hurry along this dale. The road echoes every twist and turn of the reservoir, and with an erratic slope on one side and a wandering wall on the other it is unwise to rush at the bends. Better, in fact, to take one of the many footpaths above the water, savouring the fine spread of it and of the interwoven hills beyond.

Unexpectedly, swerving round a church tower and churchyard wall, we are in the centre of Ramsgill—a few cottages, a village hall, the *Yorke Arms* hotel which was once a hunting lodge, and, of all things, peacocks strutting on the village green and posing on a cottage porch.

Eugene Aram was born in Ramsgill and, self-taught, became local schoolmaster. He was respected by his pupils as a severe disciplinarian, stern and devout in his religion. But it seems that his extramural activities included thieving and receiving stolen property. With a fellow rogue, a flax-dresser by trade, he murdered a shoemaker in Knaresborough in February 1744 and robbed him of his wife's dowry; but, having been seen, decided to leave his wife and children and flee the district. He lived for some years in Nottingham and London, and then took up a teaching post in Norfolk, where in due course he was recognized by a visitor from Knaresborough. Brought home to Yorkshire and confronted by his wife and surviving children, he is reported as saying merely, 'Well, how do you do?' He was publicly hanged at York in 1759. His adventures were romantically re-shaped in a novel by Bulwer Lytton, and also provided Thomas Hood with the inspiration for a poem.

The road from Ramsgill continues through Lofthouse but finally runs out of breath up the steep slope into Middlesmoor. Lofthouse, small as it is, has two memorial fountains of the First World War, one of them enjoining:

> *If you want to be healthy, wealthy and stout,*
> *Use plenty of cold water inside and out.*
> *Let animal and man drink freely.*

Eugene Aram married Anna Spence in the church at Middlesmoor. They had seven children: one daughter was baptized and buried here. Burials in this churchyard seem to have put bereaved families to a mighty test. The huge gravestones are inscribed with ornate lettering expressing ornate sentiments, some of them in the most florid verse. Obviously nobody dared to make do with simple names and dates, or a perfunctory 'Not lost but gone before': nothing less than twenty lines would suffice.

Middlesmoor is about as far as one can go along Nidderdale. To the north are moors and ridges and lonely reservoirs, until one comes down again upon the fertile banks and agreeable hamlets of Wensleydale. To the west, Great Whernside and more rolling moors, honeycombed with caves. Thousands of acres in the West Riding around Malham were given to the monks of Fountains Abbey in the twelfth century and used for sheep ranching. Their contours, sketched out by drystone walls, have altered little in the intervening centuries.

The abbey itself lies in much less stark surroundings, rich and expansive in the wooded shelter of Skeldale many miles to the east. A number of monks disgusted with the laxity of their Benedictine order in York came here in 1132, making a clearing in what was then thick forest, and quarried local gritstone to build an abbey where strict Cistercian rules should apply. The gift of vast sheep-walks appears to have done the grateful community more harm than good. They added to their magnificent buildings, prospered in the wool trade, and eventually were living far more luxuriously than the brethren they had so ascetically abandoned. It was ironically fitting that they should be one of the first to fall victim to Henry VIII's greed.

In the eighteenth century the abbey ruins and grounds were incorporated in the grounds of neighbouring Studley Royal. A deer park lies between the abbey and the village, and the whole now spreads out over a superb landscape of gardens, river and ornamental lakes. Within the park is the village church, built last century in a style owing much to the fourteenth century. It has a soaring spire over 150-foot high, stone and ironwork birds in its west doorway, and a mosaic floor within. There are walls of alabaster, and the first Marquis of Ripon and his wife are buried in a chapel sheltered behind a marble and alabaster screen.

Somewhat humbler is the village of Aldfield near by, its little eighteenth-century chapel filled with box pews. But it produced a distinguished son—W. P. Frith, painter of *Derby Day*.

The past history of Yorkshire settlements can be studied in several well-organized museums. In the West Yorkshire Folk Museum at Shibden Hall, Halifax, open from April to October, a fifteenth-century half-timbered house has been evocatively furnished with material from the seventeenth and eighteenth centuries. The outbuildings include an old barn and contain agricultural implements and workshops complete with craftsmen's tools. At Hutton-Le-Hole, near Farndale's wild daffodil reserve, the Ryedale Folk Museum displays collections of prehistoric and Roman finds, together with domestic equipment of three hundred years. In the grounds are a blacksmith's shop, a glass furnace, a long house from the Middle Ages and other relics of village life. And at Cliffe Castle on the outskirts of Keighley are examples of local bygones and craft workshops, with plenty of references to the local woollen industry.

In spite of the fluctuations of trade, the challenge of imported cotton and the development of synthetic fibres, it is still difficult to escape the subject of wool and cloth in the towns and villages on either side of the Pennines. In Dent, near Whernside, everybody was at it through the seventeenth and eighteenth centuries. Caps and hosiery were so unrelentingly knitted by men, women and children at their firesides or on little verandas outside their cottages that the villagers became known as 'the terrible knitters of Dent'. A re-creation of one of the outer galleries graces one of the cottages to-day. Planted in the writhing, lurching, cobbled main street as if to pin it down is a memorial fountain of Shap granite in honour of the son of a local vicar and schoolmaster: Adam Sedgwick, born here in 1785, was dubbed 'Robin Goodfellow' because of his love of the countryside and the open air, and in 1818 became professor of geology at Cambridge.

A working museum of the textile trade is being built up within a salvaged mill at Helmshore in Lancashire. In 1789 William Turner opened Higher Mill in the 'golden valley' of Rossendale, and the village of grey slate roofs grew as his profits grew. Turner was a tyrant and a slave-driver, and soon made himself a fortune. In 1826 rioters smashed over a hundred of his looms, but the mill continued to operate, and was closed down only a few years ago. Steps have been taken to preserve its essential features, to keep its machinery in working order, and to record the reminiscences of people living to-day who spent their working lives in it. From Turner's time to our own, everyone was expected to keep his nose to the grindstone, and nothing was wasted. The tyrant himself devised a foolproof time-clock which the night-watchman could not cheat—though one tried to train his dog to operate it. And one-time operatives recall that well into this century a characteristic sight in the village street was a row of large crocks outside front doors: urine was a valuable agent in cleansing fabric during processing, and the villagers were paid a penny a pot for what might be called their domestic output.

While we were in Dent we might have had a look at the little contingent of box pews in the church. These, decorated with in-dividual monograms outlined in brass-headed nails, were the preserve of the Statesmen of Dent. Descendants of yeomen who had succeeded in establishing their independence of any manorial lord after Henry VIII's destruction of monastic privileges, these 'statesmen' are to be found as local administrators across much of the Furness region. They continued to prosper from the sheep ranches, as the abbeys had once done; but in Furness they tried to move the main trading centre from Dalton to the village of Hawkshead. Although this became an important wool market, feeding many of its products to the larger town of Kendal, it somehow failed to become a thriving town itself. It had a grammar school, at which William Wordsworth was a pupil, and an imposing parish church of St Michael; it had its market and several regular fairs; but by the beginning of this century its trade had withered away. What remains is an erratic little grid of lanes and squares, a flicker of white cottages with battleship-grey slate roofs which somehow always look moist, and a disused Court House which has been leased from the National Trust as a Lake District museum. The National Trust have in fact acquired several buildings in the village and many attractive acres and lake viewpoints around it.

They have been equally assiduous in caring for the environs of Wordsworth's own village, Grasmere. The poet and his sister came to this lakeside spot in 1798 and took a cottage then called Town End, now Dove Cottage. Wordsworth married in 1801 and, for reasons usually connected with his growing family, moved house several times, ending up a few miles away at Rydal. He was often visited by Coleridge, Southey and other friends and admirers; and at one stage Thomas de Quincey took over Dove Cottage. Wordsworth, his sister and Hartley Coleridge are all buried in St Oswald's churchyard. The museum near Dove Cottage, open from April to October, has displays of rural and village life in the poet's time. There can be quite a clash between the arty and the hearty each August, when Grasmere Sports attract a great inflow of spectators and contestants for Cumberland and Westmorland wrestling, fell racing and hound trailing.

Between the peaks of the Lake District and those of the Pennines lies the vale of Eden, a most unparadisal tract when the bone-chilling 'helm wind' bites down from Melmerby Fell and Cross Fell, which rises to almost three thousand feet. Where the road begins to climb the barricade is Melmerby, an isolated little settlement until the track over Hartside Height was widened in the last century to carry traffic to Alston and the lead-mining centre of Allendale Town.

Melmerby looks warm in spite of its wind, with its red sandstone. A stream flows through its village green, and there is what appears to be a rather jolly, frivolously battlemented church tower with a gilt-figured clock face. On closer inspection this proves to be the village school, with the schoolmistress's home built in.

The drystone walls on the moors above make a tighter cross-hatching than usual. They delineate allotments provided for the miners during the nineteenth-century campaign to persuade people not to crowd into the bulging industrial towns and cities. Lead and silver have been mined on these heights for many hundreds of years, leaving behind a débris of stone ruins, chimneys and flues. Some of the most rewarding pits were those around Alston, the highest market town in England. Their gradual decline reduced Allendale Town to village status.

Well over beyond Allendale, beside the River Derwent where it forms the boundary between County Durham and Northumberland, is the sturdy stone-walled, slab-roofed village of Blanchland. The present layout owes a lot to the needs of the mining industry, but basically follows the shape of monastic buildings begun in the twelfth century. Remains of the original Premonstratensian foundation were adapted by the trustees of Lord Crewe, Bishop of Durham —responsible also for the remodelling of Bamburgh—to accommodate miners working for the estate. Houses of brown-tinged stone almost enclose a homely square, with the post office incorporated into the old abbey gatehouse, and the *Lord Crewe Arms* taking over the old storehouse. Long ago there was a watermill, built by the monks where the bridge now crosses the Derwent.

The further north we go, the less cosy and the more fundamental the villages become. We tend to think vaguely of Hadrian's Wall as being the great historic bastion against the Picts and Scots; but in fact a vulnerable slice of Cumbria and the greater part of Northumberland lie north of the escarpment along which the Romans built their stockade, watch-towers and garrison towns. Settlements along the Welsh border declined when their defensive rôle was ended; settlements here suffered not from the ailments of senility but from repeated attack during Scottish wars and border raids. There was neither the time nor the wealth to build sumptuous churches. And such churches and parsonages as did get erected had to be equipped with defensive towers, since the Scots were not above carrying off the parson along with any other loot that came to hand.

After the débâcle of Bannockburn, the fortifying of manor houses and other vulnerable buildings was intensified. The characteristic defences of the Border, still to be found in a whole string of outpost villages, were the bastle and the pele tower. A bastle or 'bastille' house was usually the home of someone of importance in the neighbourhood—someone who could not hope to withstand a protracted siege, but whose reinforced manor would protect his family until employees and neighbours could come to the rescue. A pele, from the Latin *palus*—a stake—was originally an enclosure within a stockade, but the term came to denote the actual building rather than the space within. These keeps were usually thick-walled, near cubes, with two storeys: if there was time to drive cattle in, they were kept on the ground floor, while human beings got up to the first floor, usually through a door halfway up the wall, as in east-coast church towers used as refuges from the Danes. There are vicars' pele towers at, for example, Arnside and Great Asby in Westmorland, at Corbridge on the Tyne, and ranging far up the north-easterly slant of the Border.

Gilsland stands right upon Hadrian's Wall, which in fact drives clean through the former vicarage garden. The Gilsland pass has always been a strategically important gap: the Romans concentrated some major defences here, their trans-Pennine track of the Maiden Way crossed the Wall close by; and in the time of Henry II the estates were summarily seized from Gil, their Celtic lord, and given to a reliable Norman knight who lost no time in murdering the man he had usurped. In the eighteenth century the natural sulphur and chalybeate springs turned the place into a little spa, and it was while holidaying here in 1797 that Walter Scott became engaged to Charlotte Margaret Carpenter at the Spa Hotel, now a convalescent home for miners. The only warlike establishment still flourishing in the vicinity is the Spadeadam rocket research station on the moors to the north.

In the dangerous heart of what was once No-Man's-Land, and is now the Northumberland National Park, Elsdon is a trim picture of eighteenth-century grey stone defensively enclosing a green so large it might better be called a common, with an old cattle pound. There are earthworks of a Norman motte and bailey, and a pele tower and parsonage well and truly rammed together. It is abundantly clear that the present occupants can safely cultivate their garden and trees. A little way outside the village at Steng Cross is Winter's Stob gibbet, from which dangles a wooden head in gruesome memory of Willie Winter, a murderer whose corpse was hung in chains here after execution in Newcastle-upon-Tyne.

At Chillingham, there is an ivy-wreathed example of a bastle in Hebburn Tower, on the site of an earlier tower house. It stands near the edge of parkland round which the public can be taken on guided tours to see the wild white cattle which survive here, the only pure descendants of the oxen which roamed the country seven hundred years ago. On the hilltop south-east of the park is an older fortification, the Iron Age earthwork of Ros Castle, cared for by the National Trust as a memorial to Viscount Grey of Fallodon. It was for the powerful Border family of the Greys that another chunky bastle was built at Doddington, the last one of its kind, in 1584, now looking self-consciously like a tall barn in the middle of cottages and farm buildings. Here, too, there are Iron Age remnants on Dod Law, with some strange symbols carved into the surrounding rock.

'The most dangerous spot in England'—so Norham was once described. It was certainly perilously close to the Scots, facing them from the south bank of the River Tweed. The shape of the village today is recognizably medieval, centred on the church and green, but its origins go back to the days of Celtic missionaries. A huge Norman keep was raised for its protection, and the Bishop of Durham tried to make it a borough, but failed. Village and castle are joined now by a wavering main street which, if straightened out, would almost suggest a triumphal processional route from the village green and cross to the fortress ruins. It is a wonder that so much has survived, when one considers the number of raids and sieges this defiant little place has endured. Some of its stormy past is recounted in Scott's *Marmion*, the wayward lord who met his death on Flodden Field.

That battle is commemorated just outside the village of Branxton by a cross dedicated to 'the brave of both nations' who died in 1513. There was many another battle, many an official and unofficial war, before the Border ceased to be a dangerous region in which to live. And now, in the twentieth century, there is mounting talk about Scottish independence. Border raids and pitched battles seem unlikely. No parson is going to take urgent steps to rebuild his pele tower. Is it just conceivable that there will be police and immigration officials on either side of the Tweed, and a Customs checkpoint in Norham?

CHAPTER EIGHT

Change and Decay?

On Barbury, high on the Wiltshire Downs, is a sarsen stone with the inscription:

Richard Jefferies
1848–1887
It is eternity now.
I am in the midst
of it. It is about
me in the sunshine.

The stone faces towards Jefferies' birthplace near Coate Water, where he sailed his home-made boat and absorbed the experiences which later led to his writing *Bevis, the Story of a Boy.* The lake is now a Swindon Corporation reservoir, part of it being maintained as a wildfowl reserve.

From his struggling journalistic life in London, Jefferies looked back and began to understand the richness of his country upbringing. He gave up any attempt to become a popular novelist and set about transcribing the true story of field, village and rural craftsmanship. He wrote about the wheelwright who as a matter of course became the local builder and odd job man; of the village blacksmith whose fame spread so far beyond his forge that 'gentlemen residing in the market towns send out their horses to be shod'; and of the travelling tinker at work 'on his small portable anvil, with two or three cottagers' children—sturdy, yellow-haired youngsters—intently watching the mystery of the craft'. Today they would probably be indoors watching television. Even by Jefferies' time the blacksmith was having to cope with repairing 'new-fangled machines', and there were other signs of change:

In the autumn after the harvest the gleaning is still an important time to the cottager, though nothing like it used to be. Reaping by machinery has made rapid inroads, and there is not nearly so much left behind as in former days. Yet half the women and children of the place go out and glean, but very few now bake at home; they have their bread from the baker, who comes round in the smallest hamlets. Possibly they had a more wholesome article in the olden time, when the wheat from their gleanings was ground at the village mill, and the flour made into bread at home. But the cunning of the mechanician has invaded the ancient customs; the very sheaves are now to be bound with wire by the same machine that reaps the corn. The next generation of country folk will hardly be able to understand the story of Ruth.

Ten years before Jefferies' death another chronicler of local ways, including the clamorous life of Swindon and its railway works, was born in the village of South Marston—

altogether a model village. This was brought about by a beneficent landlord, who came a stranger, and sympathised with the poor; he had all the ruinous cottages removed and filled their places with substantial modern dwellings. Nearly every cottage has gardens and parterre in front; these the occupants tend with great pride and care, vying with each other in the production of beautiful blooms.

Son and grandson of local carpenters, Alfred Williams was no happier than Jefferies with much so-called progress. But they were both shrewd countrymen at heart, whatever their streaks of sentimentality. For many a villager, 'substantial modern dwellings'—and the widening choice of modern devices which went with them— were far more attractive than the most picturesque old cottage. Jefferies might truly say that the village cobbler, 'having lived among them all his life, understands what is wanted better than the artisan of the cities'; but he and Williams knew, each in his turn, that the old order was changing and that their task was to leave as faithful a record as possible of the past on which the present is built.

Alfred Williams lived on through the First World War until 1930, and is fittingly commemorated on the other side of the Barbury stone.

Have the changes occurring since their days utterly destroyed what they would have understood as a village?

Many a smithy has become an ornamental ironwork shop for tourists. The carpenter, if there be one, is probably employed by a firm of builders and decorators operating impersonally over a wide area. If he tries to struggle along on his own because of some family tradition and pride, he will most likely be defeated by the sheer amount of paperwork imposed by tax men, Customs men and the social security offices on anyone impertinent enough to attempt independence.

Yet it is absurd to hope for a return to that never-never land of rosy-cheeked cottagers happy in their daily toil, touching their fore-locks to a beneficent squire, asking no more than the simple joys of market day, the annual fair, and dancing round the maypole on the village green. Even those who would genuinely be content with the simple life are denied it. Increasing numbers of villages owe their continuing existence to prosperous weekenders or retired people whose longing for a country cottage has inflated house prices until it has become impossible for natives to buy a home in their own birthplace—least of all the young married couples on whose future that of the entire community depends. At the same time, take away the city money that is spent in the village shop and pub, and the place might still wither away.

There are well over a thousand identifiable deserted village sites in England, and could be two or three times that many virtually 'lost'—lost, that is, until some wanderer stumbles over a puzzling mound or the footings of a building long since overgrown. We have seen that plague, enclosure, and the lure of the towns have all played their part in the sad tale of decay and emigration. Is there any reason to suppose that such processes have now ceased; that in our en-lightened, scientifically ordered twentieth century no community is in danger of social or economic fluctuations, or outright extinction?

Tell that to the people of Imber, on Salisbury Plain. Evacuated during the Second World War to make way for troops in battle training, they were promised a return to their homes when victory was won. Thirty years later the troops and tanks are still there.

Villagers are allowed back on sufferance, on high days and holidays only, or for a very occasional church service, mainly for those who once lived there or have relatives buried in the churchyard.

Tell it to the inhabitants of Donington-on-Bain in the Lincolnshire Wolds. The village was once on a railway line, but track and station disappeared long ago. I wonder if their removal was accompanied, as it has been in so many rural areas, by the promise that such abolition would be sanctioned only if adequate bus services were supplied instead? Communities which have accepted such assurances have lived to regret it. Donington had two bus services until 1 April 1973, when both were axed. A third of the villagers have no car—and after the fuel crisis later that year, one cannot in any case be too confident about the reliability of a private car—and the nearest bus stop is now three miles away. But in a place of just over two hundred people, there is no powerful pressure group and their votes for local or national elections are hardly worth soliciting. With a bit of luck the next generation will quit and go off to the towns. It really is too much trouble to keep such backwaters joined to the mainstream.

'The sheep do eat up the men': that was the cry when enclosures drove the peasants from their fields, and could well have been the symbolic cry when the textile mills drew yet more men away from the land. Now, ironically, the hedges which caused so much distress are in their turn being destroyed. Mechanized agriculture aims at using more machinery with fewer operatives, and functions to best effect over wide, uninterrupted spaces. Hedges and ditches are an expensive interruption. With the aid of Government grants, farmers have been tearing up at least 5,000 miles of hedgerow a year since the 1950s; and some would put the figure as high as 15,000 miles. And so, in the ecological chain, cottage gardens will no longer be visited by the varieties of butterfly we once knew. And great tracts of denuded English farmland may yet emulate the American dust-bowl, and inundations such as that at Santon Downham centuries ago may be repeated sooner than we think.

Another victim is the village pond. It has been estimated that as many as a hundred a week are disappearing, filled in to provide fresh agricultural land, used as the local rubbish dump, or simply allowed to silt up. It is true that the pond's practical use is less than it was: there are few coach or farm horses needing to pause for refreshment, and while most of us could think of some village scold who deserves the punishment of the ducking stool, modern juridical practice makes no provision for such sentences; while piped mains water and efficient drainage and irrigation have robbed it of other old functions. But a village robbed of its pond, like a village robbed of its green, is inevitably misshapen. Its character has been defaced, its memory blurred; and the wildlife which plays its part in the delicate balance of nature—fish, beetles, herbs and birds—has been lost from this 'outdoor classroom', as one conservationist has called it.

The Save the Village Pond Campaign is trying to halt the rot. The Conservation Corps, the Nature Conservancy, the Soil Association, and many local councils and voluntary organizations preach and practise the need to keep even the smallest cells in the body of the country healthy. The National Trust acts as guardian not only of incomparable open spaces but also of buildings, streets, and whole sections of certain villages.

Constant vigilance! It is rather a lot to ask of the ordinary man and woman with a living to earn, and a life to live. Few have the time to carry on protracted campaigns against random destruction or against faceless bureaucracy, and fewer still have the money to pay for expert advice and essential publicity. Yet in every community there may come a time when its members, harassed just once too often or contemptuously ignored for just too long, realize they are indeed a community and must act decisively if they wish to remain so. When the villagers of Upshire realized that the M16 motorway was going to make a mess of Epping Forest in their immediate neighbourhood, they collaborated in the sticking-up of posters drawing the attention of passing motorists to the attractive view about to be ruined, and collected thousands of signatures for a petition. It was somewhere near here that Boadicea was supposed to have launched one of her fiercest attacks against the Romans—the ghosts of herself and her daughters have frequently been reported on the earthwork of Amesbury Banks in the forest—and on their way to hand in the petition at Westminster the village action group stopped at the queen's statue by the Thames so that the milkman and pub landlady might lay a corn dolly wreath. There was no sign of work on the projected motorway when I last drove through Epping Forest, but one doubts whether even the most courageous villagers, with all the right in the world on their side, can hold it off for ever.

Yet, commendable as it is to preserve all that is both good and preservable from our past, stubborn conservatism can be as absurd as the worst vandalism. We are living in the present and have to cope with it and at the same time steer towards a feasible future. This does not mean converting the village shop into a chain store without a struggle, installing a fruit machine in the fifteenth-century inn, or converting Jacobean almshouses into a motel. It does mean making the best of things; and I mean making the best, not merely making do.

Below the village of Atwick in East Yorkshire is being installed an underground gasometer capable of holding 4000 million cubic feet of North Sea gas. Caverns gouged out of the unique rock salt formations under Atwick will be used to store natural gas from the offshore fields as a reserve to meet peak demands. There was a time when such a scheme would have been carried through without any attempt at local consultation. In this case, British Gas officials and technicians paid repeated visits to the village to explain the process, to reassure those afraid of leakages, and to discuss all reasonable questions and requests about construction work and later operation.

At Drax, near Selby, a new coal-fired power station will be largely fuelled from an automated drift mine capable of producing ten million tons a year for at least fifty years. This is not all that far from the better known coalfields of the Pontefract area, but hitherto has been a predominantly rural plain dotted with farming hamlets. It is hoped to keep it that way. No untreated spoil heaps, and no gaunt pit-head workings. Farmers around Ryther were concerned about possible subsidence; but other residents see a brighter future for the village, which has consistently suffered from poor water pressure, unreliable electricity supply, no gas, no shops and no bus service. The village school has struggled on with difficulty. 'A coal mine,' said the clerk to the parish council in June 1974, 'certainly couldn't do us any harm'. The pit-head will probably be sited near the village of Hambleton, and the Coal Board has made it clear that intelligent landscaping is high on its scale of priorities: a neighbouring Forestry Commission plantation may be used to mask the drift-head constructions, and if there are to be changes in the life style of the region, those changes must be calculated for the better.

There are lessons to be learned from across the Border. The outline plan announced in mid-1974 for a new town at Stonehouse in Lanarkshire proposed that it should comprise a number of separate villages, each with a population of between three and six thousand and each with its own nursery school, shops and recreation area, linked to a town centre with a main shopping complex, offices and schools. Such concepts augur well for the future. After all, even in London one repeatedly comes across people who talk of their 'village' —Canonbury, for example, and Clerkenwell, parts of South Kensington and scores of little enclaves in the East End, the bit of Marylebone around New Cavendish Street, Highgate ... There is still a human longing to see things on a human scale.

Julius Caesar is quoted as having said he 'had rather be first in a village than second at Rome'. This may be read as a dictatorial aspiration along the lines of the well-known frog and the little pond. But it could more charitably be interpreted as I have known it tacitly interpreted and put into effect by many craftsmen and other servants of the parish: as a man's unboastful consciousness of his own worth and what he can best contribute to the community in which he chooses to live.

There will be healthy and prosperous villages so long as there are men and women willing to make them and keep them so. And if this will should be lost ... why, then the streets and houses, church and green and pump and pub have lost all meaning anyway.

Bibliography

BONHAM-CARTER, VICTOR, *The English Village* (Pelican, 1952)

BRAUN, HUGH, *Old English Houses* (Faber, 1962)

CLIFTON-TAYLOR, ALEC, *The Pattern of English Building* (Faber, 1972)

EVANS, GEORGE EWART, *The Farm and the Village* (Faber, 1969)

FINBERG, J., *Exploring Villages* (Routledge & Kegan Paul, 1958)

FLEURE, H. J., & DAVIES, M., *Natural History of Man in Britain* (Fontana, 1971)

HIGGS, JOHN, *The Land* (Studio Vista, 1964)

HOSKINS, W. G., *The Making of the English Landscape* (Hodder & Stoughton, 1955; Penguin, 1970)

—, *English Landscapes* (BBC Publications, 1973)

HUGGETT, FRANK E., *A Day in the Life of a Victorian Farm Worker* (Allen & Unwin, 1972)

JENNINGS, PAUL, *The Living Village* (Hodder & Stoughton, 1968; Penguin, 1972)

MILLS, DENNIS R., *The English Village* (Routledge & Kegan Paul, 1968)

The above is, obviously, only a brief selection. It is impossible to list all the admirable books written about the villages of different regions of England, or the various county and regional books in which villages play a substantial part. Each reader will have his or her own favourite. I must, however, draw attention to the invaluable series of 'Landscape' volumes edited by Professor Hoskins, published by Hodder & Stoughton, and each written by an expert on the area. The subject is not exclusively that of villages, but in every case one's understanding of the birth and development, or decline, of such settlements is enhanced by the author's presentation of the over-all picture.

As to autobiographies and semi-autobiographical, half-fictionalized studies of village life, there are so many that selection has again to be a matter of personal choice—or, often, of chance. I offer a mere handful of my own favourites. Of these, Flora Thompson's classic trilogy must surely be on everybody's list.

BLYTHE, RONALD, *Akenfield* (Allen Lane, 1969; Penguin, 1972)

KENDON, FRANK, *The Small Years* (Cambridge University Press, 1930)

KETTERIDGE, C., & MAYS, S., *Five Miles from Bunkum* (Eyre Methuen, 1972)

MITFORD, MARY RUSSELL, *Our Village* (Everyman's Library, Dent, frequently reprinted)

THOMPSON, FLORA, *Lark Rise to Candleford* (Oxford University Press, World's Classics, 1971; Penguin, 1973)

Index

The numerals in italics refer to the figure numbers of the illustrations

Index

Index

Index

Index

Index